Revised and Updated Edition

The Expansion of Islam

A Nineteenth-Century Treatise
by Sami Frashëri

Also by Flamur Vehapi

The Book of Great Quotes, 2025 (2nd ed.)
Berke Khan of the Golden Horde, 2024
The World According to Sami Frashëri, 2024
Kosovo: A Brief Chronology, 2023
Verses of the Heart: Poems, 2021
Ertugrul Ghazi: A Very Short Biography, 2021
The Book of Albanian Sayings: Cultural Proverbs, 2017
Peace and Conflict Resolution in Islam, 2016
A Cup with Rumi: Poems, 2015
The Alchemy of Mind: Poems, 2008, 2016
Sfidat Jetike: Poezi, 2002

Translations

The Expansion of Islam by Sami Frashëri, 2025 (2nd ed.)
The Album of Aphorisms by Sami Frashëri, 2019

The Expansion of Islam

A Nineteenth-Century Treatise
by Sami Frashëri

Translation, Introduction and Notes by
Flamur Vehapi

Foreword by
Didmar Faja

Crescent Books

© **Flamur Vehapi 2025**

The Expansion of Islam
by Crescent Books, an imprint of
Crescent Institute LLC - Portland, OR.
e-mail: crescent.books2020@gmail.com
First Edition published in 2019
Current edition published in 2025

All rights reserved.
No part of this publication may be reproduced,
stored in any retrieval system, or transmitted,
in any form or by any means, electronic,
mechanical, photocopying, recording or otherwise
without the prior written permission of the publisher and/or the author.

Prepared and Typeset
by Erzen Pashaj
Maps by Arbnor Rashiti

Paperback
ISBN: 978-1-954935-11-2
Second English edition, fully revised and updated.
Title of the original work:
همة الهمم في نشر الإسلام

Includes biographical references and appendices.
Text copy edited by Stella Williams.
Cover design by Stella Williams.
Published in the United States of America

To my beloved parents,
my siblings, and to
Suhail and Ryanne,
the sunshine of my world.

To the people of Palestine as well,
who have been struggling
for nearly a century to free themselves
from the shackles of colonial occupation.
#FreePalestine

Contents

Sami Frashëri's Biography	1
Works by Sami Frashëri	3
List of Maps	6
Foreword	9
Introduction	13
A Note from the Translator	15
The Treatise	19
Glossary	51
Appendices	57
Acknowledgments	75
Notes	77
Bibliography and Suggested Readings	83
About the Translator	93

Sami Frashëri's Biography

Sami Frashëri, also known as Shams al-Din Sami Frashëri,[1] was born in 1850 in the village of Frashër, Albania, to a distinguished Muslim family. His early Islamic education, alongside his brothers Naim and Abdyl, was overseen by his parents, Halit and Emine. Following their parents' deaths, Sami's older brother, Abdyl, relocated the family to Janina, where Sami attended the prestigious Zosimaia High School.[2] There, Sami mastered Greek, French, and Italian, in addition to his native Albanian.[1] Later, he added Arabic, Persian, and Turkish to his repertoire, fostering a broad linguistic and cultural knowledge.[2]

During this period, Sami's exposure to diverse personalities, books, and ideas from both Eastern and Western thought profoundly influenced him, leading to his transformation into an innovative thinker. Following his brother Naim's path, he relocated to Istanbul in 1872. While there, Sami became an exceptionally prolific writer, with a remarkable career in the

---

[1] In Turkish literature Sami is referred to as Şemseddin (or Şemsettin) Sami Bey. "Shams al-Din" is a very common name or honorific, meaning 'sun of the faith' in Arabic.

[2] The present-day city of Janina (Ioannina in Greek) was part of the Ottoman Janina Vilayet (administrative division), and its population was predominantly Albanian and Greek with Islam and Christian Orthodoxy being the major religions there. Janina was ceded to Greece in 1913 following the Balkan Wars. See McCarthy, *Death and Exile*, 1995.

Ottoman bureau of the press. He actively engaged in various community initiatives while maintaining a relentless commitment to writing. His career also led him to brief postings in Libya in 1874 and Rhodes in 1877.[3] Additionally, he held positions as chief editor for several journals and newspapers within the Ottoman Empire.[3]

Sami gained recognition for authoring the first modern historical and geographical dictionary of the Ottoman Empire. Alongside that, it's said that he authored over fifty books in multiple languages, although many of them are regrettably lost to history, and others remain untranslated. His accessible work and brief biographies underscore his reputation as a remarkable scholar and polymath.[4]

Sami is often compared to figures like Muhammad Iqbal and Jamal al-Din al-Afghani, who similarly sought to awaken their communities through education, cultural revival, and reform. Like Iqbal, Sami emphasized the power of national identity and intellectual progress, inspiring his people with philosophical and literary works. Comparable to Al-Afghani, Sami used his writings to bridge tradition and modernity, advocating for unity and resisting societal stagnation. Not surprisingly, historians often rightfully regard Sami as a key figure in shaping modern Albanian identity. All three shared a vision of empowering their communities by blending Islamic values with the transformative power of knowledge and modern ideas.

Sami passed away in 1904 in Istanbul at the age of 54, leaving behind his wife Emine and five children.[5] Today, his legacy endures, with his name and works celebrated among Albanian- and Turkish-speaking communities worldwide.[6]

---

[3] A few sources claim that Sami was instead banished to Libya and Rhodes during this period due to his writings and political involvements, but later was granted an imperial pardon. See Charles Kurzman, editor, *Modernist Islam, 1840-1940*, 149-151, 2002. Elsie makes no mention of this. See Elsie, *Albanian Literature*, 78, 2005.

Works by Sami Frashëri

Some of Sami Frashëri's works include the following:

Drama (Turkish)
- *Besâ yâhut Âhde Vefâ* (Besa or The Given Word of Trust), 1874.
- *Seydi Yahya*, 1875.[7]
- *Gâve* (Gave the Blacksmith), 1876.
- *Mezalim-i Endülûs* (Atrocities in Andalusia), never printed.
- *Vicdân* (Conscience), never printed.

Novels (Turkish)
- *Ta'aşşûk-ı Tal'at ve Fitnât* (The Love Between Talat and Fitnat), 1873.

Language studies and linguistics
- *Usûl-ü Tenkîd ve Tertîb* (Orthography of Turkish), 1886.
- *Nev-usûl Sarf-ı Türkî* (Modern Turkish Grammar), 1891.
- *Yeni Usûl-ü Elifbâ-yı Türkî* (New Turkish Alphabetical System), 1898.
- *Usûl-ü Cedîd-i Kavâ'id-i 'Arabiyye* (New Method for Learning Arabic), 1910. *Tatbîkât-ı 'Arabiyye* (Language Exercises in Arabic), 1911.

Dictionaries and encyclopedias
- *Kamûs-ı Fransevî* (French-Turkish dictionary), 1882–1905.
- *Kamûs-ı Fransevî* (French-Turkish dictionary), 1885.
- *Küçük Kamûs-ı Fransevî* (French-Turkish dictionary), 1886.
- *Kamûs-ul Alâm* (Universal Dictionary or Encyclopedia of General Science), 6 volumes, 1889–1899.
- *Kamûs-ı 'Arabî* (Arabic-Turkish dictionary), unfinished, 1898.
- *Kamus-ı Türki* (Dictionary of the Classical Ottoman Turkish language), 2 volumes, 1899–1900. This work is widely used to this day.

Educational writings (Albanian)
- *Alfabetarja e Stambollit* (The Alphabet of Istanbul), 1879.
- *Abetarja e Shkronjëtorja* (The ABC Book and the Place of Writing), a work of grammar, 1886.

Scientific writings (Albanian)
- *Qielli* (The Sky)
- *Toka* (The Earth)
- *Njeriu* (The Human Being)
- *Gjuha* (The Language)

Political works (attributed to Sami)
- *Shqipëria ç'ka qenë, ç'është e çdo të bëhet* (Albania, What It Was, What It Is and What It Will Be), 1899.[4]

---

[4] Widely used by Albanian political nationalists as their "nationalist manifesto," it should be noted that a number of sources have disputed the authorship of this work, as it does not align with the legacy of Sami and the rest of his writings. First published in Bucharest, Romania, this work originally had no indication of the author or the publisher. See Bilmez, "Shemseddin Sami Frashëri" in *We, the People*, edited by Mishkova, 341-371, 2009; Elsie, *Historical Dictionary of Albania*, 2010; Misha, "Invention of a Nationalism …" in *Albanian Identities: Myth and History*, edited by Schwandner-Sievers and Fischer, 2002.

Other Works

In his "Pocket Library" (in Turkish), Frashëri published historical and scientific booklets on the following subjects:

1. History of Islam and Islamic civilization (including *Medeniyyet-i Islamiyye*, 1879 and *Himmetül-Himem fi Neshril-Islam,* 1884/5 (1302 AH) by Mihran Matbaası, Istanbul)
2. Astronomy
3. Geology
4. Anthropology
5. Mythology
6. Aphorisms and more.

He also published collections of proverbs, quotes, and humor, many of which are still accessible and referenced today in the Albanian- and Turkish-speaking worlds.

THE EXPANSION OF ISLAM

List of Maps

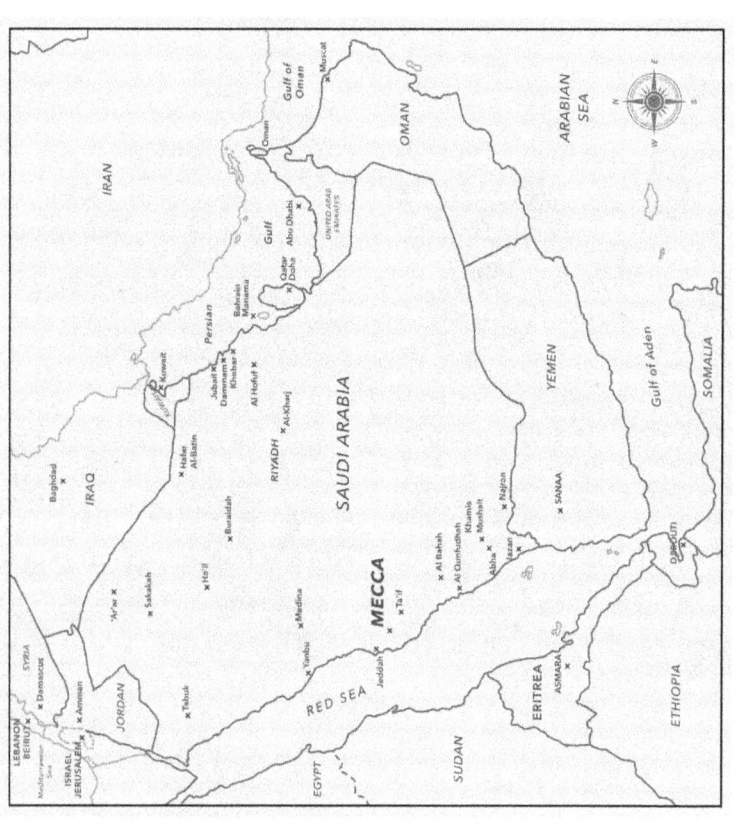

Fig. 1. The Arabian Peninsula.

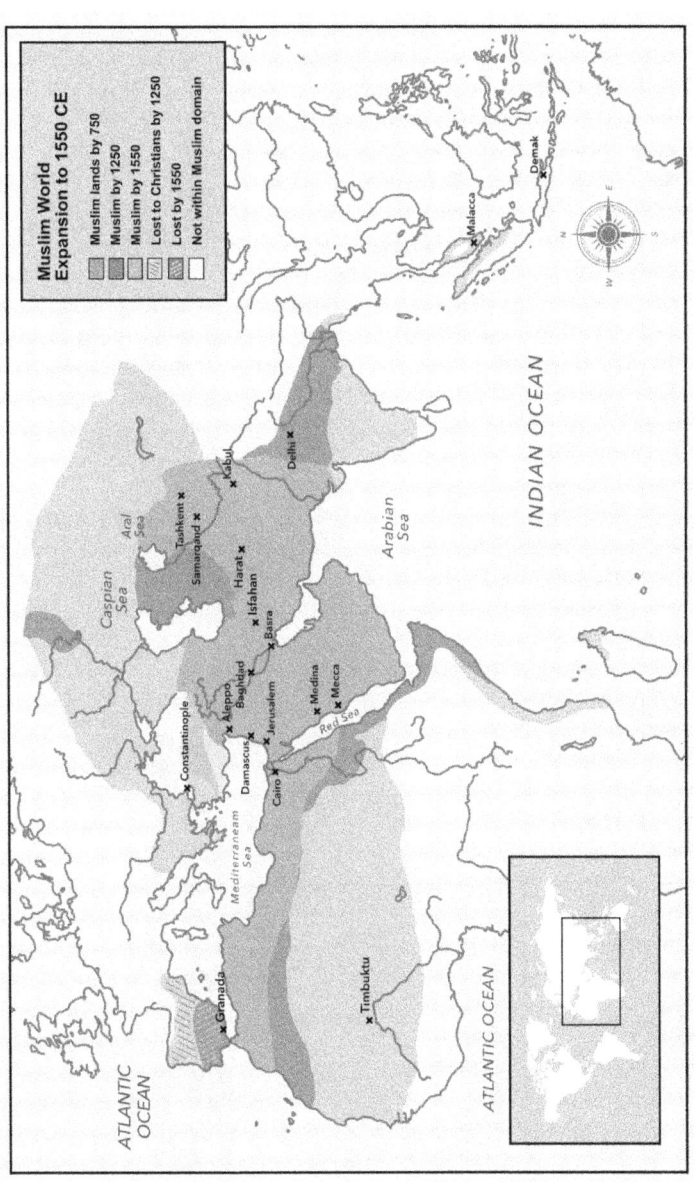

Fig. 2. The expansion of Islam to 1500 CE.

Foreword

It is with great honor and enthusiasm that I write this foreword for the translated work of *The Expansion of Islam* by Sami Frashëri, known in the Muslim world as Shams al-Din Sami Frashëri. This masterful translation by Flamur Vehapi brings to a wider audience one of the most concise yet profound summaries of the history of the Islamic world. Sami Frashëri, a 19th-century Albanian Ottoman scholar, philosopher, lexicographer, and polymath, has left an indelible mark on both Ottoman and Albanian intellectual history.

Renowned for his scholarly contributions, Sami Frashëri stood as a defender of Albanian rights while serving as a bridge between cultures and languages. His most celebrated work, *Kāmūsu'l A'lām*, the Encyclopedia of General Science, remains a testament to his erudition, marking the first printed encyclopedia in Ottoman Turkish. Despite his claim of limited proficiency in the Arabic language, Frashëri's work reflects a deep appreciation for its importance, particularly in understanding Islamic texts and history

This book is not merely a historical account; it is a narrative woven with insights into how Islam has shaped individuals, societies, and civilizations. Frashëri eloquently highlights the peaceful spread of Islam, dispelling misconceptions about its growth. He states, "It is likely that the global Muslim population is far higher than what geographers and historians project. This is because Islam grows rapidly without force or fighting."

Frashëri's historical analysis demonstrates how Islam eradicated many harmful practices, where, in certain parts of the world, the faith abolished the custom of burning widows alive, among other injustices. He does not confine his observations to religious matters alone but also emphasizes the role of Islam in advancing natural and rational sciences alongside religious ones. This dual contribution to human knowledge underscores the holistic nature of Islamic civilization.

In his writing, Frashëri highlights how Islam transforms society: "Islam purifies morality through its strong foundation, such as obligatory prayers, charity, honoring the guest, and safeguarding the traveler. It sows justice, equality, and sincerity in the hearts of people. It teaches rulers that, like those they govern, they also have duties and responsibilities to fulfill. It builds societies on sound foundations, deters tyrants with God-consciousness, and consoles the afflicted and the poor with mercy, promises of His reward, and felicity in the

Hereafter." Frashëri's insights into Islamic unity are particularly striking. He underscores the importance of adherence to the central authority of Muslims, represented during his time by the Ottoman Sultan, as a means to foster unity and strength. His reflections on the geographical, cultural, and linguistic diversity of Muslim societies provide a snapshot of the Islamic world during his lifetime, making this work invaluable for understanding the rich tapestry of Muslim civilization.

The translation of this essential work by Flamur Vehapi ensures that Sami Frashëri's timeless wisdom reaches contemporary audiences, offering both inspiration and education. Vehapi's dedication to preserving the authenticity and elegance of the original text while making it accessible to English readers is a commendable achievement.

May this translation serve as a bridge between past and present, East and West, fostering greater understanding of the rich history and enduring contributions of Islam to humanity. It is my hope that readers will find in this work not only a history of Islam but also a celebration of the faith's profound impact on the human experience.

— **Mufti Didmar Faja**, author of *Echoes of the Prophet*
January 21, 2025 / Rajab 21, 1446 H

THE EXPANSION OF ISLAM

Introduction

Sami Frashëri's treatise is a significant contribution to Muslim history. It is one of the author's few works written in Arabic, first published in 1884/5 (1302 AH) in Istanbul and dedicated to the proponents of Islam.[5] Originally, this work was part of his "Cep Kütüphanesi" ("Pocket Library") series, which aimed to disseminate knowledge on various subjects in an accessible format. While concise and constructive, the treatise does contain historical gaps and discrepancies, particularly regarding timeframes, specific dates, and names of rulers. The omission aspect may stem from the author's possible assumption that his audience was already familiar with the context of the events. As a result, unfamiliar readers may find it challenging to follow, making the translator's footnotes invaluable. However, there are instances where I chose not to provide footnotes, even when it might have been appropriate, to avoid overloading this brief work with additional commentary.

Translating and presenting an old text to a modern audience is inherently challenging. A great deal of meaning is often lost in translation, and additional nuances may be overlooked when

---

[5] The year 1876 has also been cited for the original publication of this work. However, we now know that 1879 is the publication year of his other work, *Medeniyyet-i İslâmiyye*. Since both works were part of the same collection, the dates have often been confused. See Frashëri, *Vepra*. 7 vols., 2024.

shifting contexts from one historical period to another. Readers should bear in mind that recording and writing history a century ago was vastly different from contemporary practices. Standards of referencing, style, and access to information that we now take for granted did not exist. Consequently, many writers published what was considered logical and culturally acceptable at the time, without the means to verify the details. This context helps explain certain misunderstandings or biases within the text. For example, Sami's prediction that the spread of Islam in the West would be difficult, if not impossible, is clearly contradicted by present-day realities. The reader should keep in mind this is a unique snapshot of his perceptions, not necessarily reflective of the present-day realities for the people he is discussing.

Despite these inconsistencies, Sami was well-versed in Islamic history and the geopolitical affairs of his time. He demonstrated a keen understanding of the wider historical implications of colonialism, rightly affirming that, although the colonists claimed otherwise, their aim was not to assist, educate, or civilize others but to dominate and exploit them. Moreover, Sami addressed misconceptions about Islam that persist even in contemporary Western literature, dispelling myths with well-argued points.

In this concise work, he passionately reminded Muslims of both their prosperous and challenging histories, echoing the Qur'an's call for learning, growth, and active participation in society. Sami himself embodied this call to action.

Flamur Vehapi
Portland, Oregon

A Note from the Translator

Although a renowned scholar and a national prodigy, Sami Frashëri remains an overlooked figure in Western writings and, surprisingly, among Albanian nationalists as well. He is often misleadingly depicted as an isolated academic and a distant national icon, disconnected from Ottoman life and devoid of any religious sentiment or affiliation, despite being a Muslim Ottoman citizen who resided in Istanbul. These overly simplistic and sterile portrayals reduce Sami to someone who spent his life solely reflecting on the glories, struggles, and rise of the Albanian nation. However, objective historians and Sami's own life story reveal that such reductionist depictions do a great disservice to the man and his legacy.[8] While Sami certainly contributed to the Albanian national cause and wrote passionately about his homeland, this represents only a fragment of his prolific and multifaceted body of work.

First and foremost, Sami was a husband and father, an activist and intellectual, a polyglot, poet, philosopher, historian, and a practicing Sunni Muslim, as evidenced by his life and writings, particularly during the period in which he composed this treatise.[6]

---

[6] Some have argued that Sami belonged to the Bektashi order, primarily because Bektashism was and remains prevalent in the region where he was born. While his brother, Naim Frashëri, seems to indicate some preference for Bektashism in some of his writings, Sami himself never provides any hints or impressions to suggest such an affiliation. It seems that due to

Contrary to the claims of some Albanian nationalist rhetoric, which unfairly dismisses the Ottoman Empire's contributions to Albania, Sami did not harbor resentment toward the Ottomans or their rule. On the contrary, his writings reflect an acknowledgment of the Ottoman Empire's role in enriching Balkan cultures.[9] Balkan history and society further demonstrate the validity of this perspective, affirming Sami's view of the Ottoman legacy as a complement to the region's diverse heritage.[10]

In contrast to some nationalist rhetoric, much of Sami's writing is unrelated to Albania or its people, and not all of his works were written in his native Albanian language, like the treatise at hand which was written in Arabic. In terms of my translation, it was not translated directly from Arabic but rather from two main Albanian sources (listed in the Bibliography). However, I consulted Arabic and Turkish sources to ensure the accuracy of the translation. To avoid confusion—considering that both of his older brothers were also involved in similar efforts around the same timeframe—I will refer to Sami Frashëri throughout this work as Sami or the author. All notes, citations, and appendices in this work are mine. Additionally, any in-text comments in parentheses are those of Sami Frashëri or the early editors/translators, while comments in brackets are mine, added solely to aid the reader's understanding of the original text.

As the reader will note, Sami does not refer to the Gregorian calendar while discussing historical events, but the Hijri (Islamic) calendar. However, Gregorian dates have also been added in some cases to aid the reader.

---

his birthplace, family ties to Bektashism, and possible past associations with the order, Sami has often been categorized as a member. However, the evidence for these claims is insufficient and highly ambiguous. See Frashëri, *Vepra*. 7 vols., 2024.

The Hijri calendar is lunar with 12 months, and its start marks the migration (Hijrah) of the Prophet ﷺ from Makkah to Medinah. This occurred in 622 CE, marking year 1 of the Islamic calendar. To estimate the start of a particular Gregorian year (CE) in terms of the Hijrah year (AH), first deduct 622.5643 from the CE year and then multiply the result by 1.030684:

AH = 1.030684 (CE − 622.5643)

Similarly, to convert from a Hijrah year to a Gregorian year, multiply the AH year by 0.970229 and add 621.5643:

CE = 0.970229 x AH + 621.5643

For example, using the second equation for AH 1408: 1408 x 0.970229 + 621.5643 equals 1987.6467, with the decimal portion equating to seven months and twenty-four days, or 24 August. Indeed, the year AH 1408 started on 26 August 1987.[11] However, to simplify this process, there are many online converter engines available that can calculate the conversion between Gregorian and Hijrah years, and vice versa, as well as provide conversions for specific dates.

THE EXPANSION OF ISLAM

The Expansion of Islam: A Nineteenth-Century Treatise

In the name of Allah, the Beneficent, the All-Merciful!

Praise be to God, who said, "Indeed, the true religion with God is Islam" (Qur'an 3:19). May greetings and salutations of peace be upon our guide, Prophet Muhammad ﷺ, the best of creation, his family and Companions, and those who led the Muslims after them: the great caliphs, the noble leaders, and the scholars who spread the religion of the [Almighty] Creator around the world, and shared its light by means of knowledge and great sacrificial efforts. Through these means, the darkness of unbelief was lifted from [the hearts of many] people. May prayers [and salutations] be upon the leader [of the believers (*Amir al-Mu'minin*)] and their protector in the West and the East, his highness, the caliph of our time, the pride of the Ottomans, Sultan Abdul Hamid Hani, the son of Sultan Abdul Majid Hani.[12] O God, protect him, for he is the defender of the faith in every place and time, and You (O God) are the Almighty; Your help [alone] we seek!

I, the humble servant, in great need of God's mercy, Shams al-Din Sami Frashëri, write the following words.

A Treatise in Arabic

Arabic is a language for all Muslims and serves as a common scientific language among scholars.[13] For this reason, I deemed it appropriate to write this short treatise in this timeless language [Arabic], despite my limited proficiency in it, as my usual medium [of writing and scholarship] is the Turkish language.[14] Therefore, I extend my apologies to the esteemed readers for any [shortcomings,] errors, or omissions that may have occurred in the process. My intent in writing this treatise was not to showcase my knowledge or skills [in Arabic], but rather to provide a benefit to all our brothers in faith. This treatise, may God preserve it, addresses the ways in which Islam spread across various regions, the lives of Muslim communities, and the periods during which different peoples embraced Islam. The significance and value of such a treatise are self-evident, as is the necessity for it to be in the hands of every believer.

The Spread of Islam

It is natural that the emergence of Islam began among the Arabs, as our Messenger ﷺ was an Arab, and the Qur'an was revealed in Arabic.[15]

Before Islam, during the *Jahiliyyah* period,[7] the Arabs were divided into scattered tribes with no unity or means of reconciliation among themselves. Each tribe spoke its own specific language (i.e., dialect), and conflicts and wars were constant among them. With the advent of Islam, these tribes united and became one people (an *ummah*).[16] The Qur'an, revealed in their purest and most eloquent language, rendered all other dialects secondary.[17]

Initially, Islam was confined to the Arabian Peninsula until the caliphate of Umar bin al-Khattab, may God be pleased with

---

[7] The pre-Islamic age of ignorance and unbelief in Arabia. See *Glossary* at the end of this book.

him. Before [the advent of Islam], the Arabs were content with their deserts, tents, and camels, and they had never conquered foreign lands or peoples. However, after uniting and having their minds illuminated by the teachings of Islam, they gained a new spiritual power and enthusiasm. This newfound vigor made the Arabian Peninsula feel too small for them. They soon moved beyond its borders, liberating Sham, Iraq, Persia, and Khorasan,[8] followed by Egypt and [a significant portion of] Africa.[18]

At the time, many of these liberated regions were inhabited by people of diverse backgrounds, including Assyrians, Celts, Persians, Copts, and Berbers. Most of these groups, apart from the inhabitants of Persia and Khorasan, quickly assimilated and became Arabized. The Persians and Khorasanis, although retaining their cultural identity, also began adopting Arabic for their literary works after embracing Islam.[19]

The campaigns of liberation and the spread of Islam were initially temporarily delayed due to disagreements between Ali (r.a.) and Mu'awiyah (r.a.) (over the succession of the caliphate) and the tragedy at Karbala.[20] However, as the Muslim expansion continued westward, the Umayyad rulers liberated regions such as Tunisia, Algeria, and Morocco. Later, Musa bin Nusayr[9] and Tariq [ibn Ziyad] advanced into Europe, conquering Andalusia,[10]

---

[8] Sham encompassed present-day Syria, Lebanon, Jordan, and Palestine, serving as a major cultural and political center in the Islamic world. Persia, which historically referred to the Persian Empire, is now modern-day Iran, maintaining its rich cultural and historical legacy. Khorasan, once a vast and influential region, today spans eastern Iran, Afghanistan, Turkmenistan, and Uzbekistan, historically known for its contributions to Islamic scholarship and trade.

[9] Musa bin Nusayr (d. 716 CE) had served as a governor and general in the North African provinces under the Umayyad caliph Al-Walid I.

[10] Andalusia refers to a significant portion of the present-day Iberian Peninsula, where Muslims established their presence from 711 to 1492. See Thomson and 'Ata'ur-Rahim, *The Presence of Islam in Andalus*, 2023.

which now encompasses modern-day Spain and Portugal. They also extended their rule to include half of the French kingdom and many islands in the Mediterranean Sea, such as Cyprus, Crete, Sicily, and others.

Meanwhile, Muslim expansion toward the East progressed steadily. They absorbed regions like Transoxiana,[11] Khwarazm, the settlements of the Turks and Tatars, and areas like Herat, Kabul, and Kelat,[21] eventually reaching the borders of India[22] and China.[23] With the arrival of Sultan Mahmoud Sebüktegin,[12] Muslims gained control over large parts of India, incorporating even more territories into the growing [Islamic] empire.

The advent of Islam brought immense benefits to humanity. It eradicated numerous strange and harmful practices associated with disbelief. As a case in point, it abolished the custom of burning widows alive after the death of their husbands.[13] This transformative impact marked the close of the first century of Muslim expansion.[24]

Islam's Outlook after the First Century

After the fall of the Umayyad dynasty [in 750 CE], the caliphate was divided into two: the Caliphate of the East, or the Abbasid state, and the Caliphate of the Maghreb, or the Umayyad state,

---

[11] Referred to in Arabic sources as *Ma Wara' an-Nahr* ('Land Beyond the River'), this ancient name was used for a portion of Central Asia. The region roughly corresponds to present-day Uzbekistan, Tajikistan, southern Kyrgyzstan, and southwestern Kazakhstan.

[12] Here, the author refers to Yamin-ud-Dawla Abul-Qasim Mahmud ibn Sebüktegin, also known as Mahmud of Ghazni, who reigned from 998 to 1030.

[13] The tradition of burning widowed women alive, known as *suttee*, has been recorded in North India since the fourth century BCE. There are also accounts of similar practices among the Slavic peoples, Scandinavians, Greeks, Chinese, some Native American groups, and others. See Stein, "Women to Burn: Suttee as a Normative Institution," 1978.

which was established in Andalusia. At this point, Muslims ruled independently across vast territories, stretching from the Far East, at the borders of China and Transoxiana, to the Far West, reaching the Atlantic Ocean (i.e., the Maghreb). The Arabic language was widespread throughout these lands, two-thirds of which had been inhabited since antiquity.[14]

With the cessation of conquest and liberation campaigns, Muslims shifted their focus to [the development of] sciences, craftsmanship, and production. Their pursuits were not confined to religious sciences such as *tafsir*, *hadith*, *fiqh*, or the literary sciences.[15] They also advanced in the natural and rational sciences, inspired by the saying, "Seek knowledge even in China" (Hadith).[16] Muslim scholars began gathering and translating the works of Greek, Indian, and Persian thinkers into Arabic. Schools and major academies were established in Baghdad, Egypt, Bukhara, Cordoba, and many other cities and cultural hubs. Students from across the world flocked to these centers to study both traditional and rational sciences.[25] As a result, Muslim scientists and philosophers emerged, competing with—and often surpassing—the ancient Greek philosophers in fields such as philosophy, medicine, astronomy, mathematics, and the natural sciences.[26] The number of Muslim scholars who wrote in these disciplines is undoubtedly immense and far too vast to enumerate in this brief treatise.[27] Moreover, the number of those who contributed to history, literature, fiqh, and other religious sciences was significantly higher.

---

[14] As of 2024, Arabic is the native language for approximately 372 million people worldwide. Including non-native speakers, the total number of Arabic speakers rises to around 422 million. Arabic serves as an official language in 22 countries across the Middle East and North Africa.

[15] See *Glossary* at the end of this book.

[16] The grade and authenticity of this hadith have been questioned by several scholars. The authentic version appears to be: "Seeking knowledge is an obligation upon every Muslim" (*Sunan Ibn Majah*, 224).

Such was the state of Islam and Muslims during the time of the two great dynasties: the Abbasids in the East and the Umayyads in the West (Andalusia). This era lasted for about six centuries, during which science, knowledge, production, trade, and civilizational advancements were predominantly in the hands of Muslims and under the dominion of Islam.[28]

The Trials of the Muslims
The two states [the Abbasids and Umayyads] were eventually overcome by weakness and exhaustion, and their people fell on hard times. They faced relentless attacks from the armies of the unbelievers: the Mongols from the east and the Europeans from the west. [These invaders] brought destruction, pillaged cities, slaughtered innocents, and burned what they could. Only a few of the works of the Muslims survived.[17] Most of these invaders were barbaric in nature. For instance, the armies of Genghis Khan shed the blood of [many] innocent Muslim men, women, and children without any justification.[18] They destroyed everything and killed everyone in their path—people, books, and schools alike.[29]

As for the Europeans, they were deeply entrenched in ignorance at the time.[19] Their fanaticism and hatred toward Muslims were intense. However, some [European non-Muslims living under

---

[17] Some who survived the sack of Baghdad recounted that the waters of the River Tigris turned black with ink from the countless books thrown into the river. See, for instance, Arnold, *The Preaching of Islam,* 1913; Armstrong, *Islam,* 2000.

[18] The estimated number of those killed varies. Martin Sicker cites 90,000, while other sources, including Ian Frazier, suggest a significantly higher death toll, ranging from several hundred thousand to a million. See Frazier, "Invaders: Destroying Baghdad," 2005.

[19] This refers to the Dark Ages that had engulfed most of Europe, with the exception of the Iberian Peninsula. See Graham, *How Islam Created the Modern World,* 2006.

Muslim rule] may not have welcomed the collapse of Muslim rule in Andalusia,[20] since the [Catholic] friars[21] by then had established trials to "remove the devil" and forcibly convert the non-Christian populations [of Europe].[30] Muslims, along with Jews and others, who refused to cooperate (convert by force) were burned at the stake.[22] Many converted to Christianity to escape death, yet even after converting, a number were brutally killed by the orders of the church. After this ordeal, no Muslims remained in Andalusia.[31] In this manner, Muslims lost Spain, Portugal, Sicily, and their territories in France and Italy.

These horrific crimes [such as the Spanish Inquisition] did not satisfy the Europeans, however. Many gathered across Europe under the banner of the cross and launched frequent attacks on Muslim lands.[32] While they succeeded in expelling Muslims from Europe, they failed to achieve anything [significant to the Muslims] in Asia and Africa. History will forever remember these [atrocious] acts as their shameful legacy until the Day of Resurrection. This stands in stark contrast to when Muslims ruled Andalusia; they treated all with respect and governed with justice and kindness. Even Western historians have recorded and confirmed this.[33] As for the Mongols, their hostility toward Muslims was evident, and bloodshed itself was an easy and captivating pursuit for many of them.[34]

After their conquests slowed, the Mongols faced the reality of governing the lands they had conquered. Recognizing

---

[20] Many non-Muslims had no objection to Muslim rule, as they were granted a variety of inalienable rights. See Lowney, *A Vanished World*, 2006; Menocal, *The Ornament of the World*, 2002.

[21] Unlike a monk, a friar is a 'brother' or member of one of the Christian mendicant orders established during the European Middle Ages.

[22] Estimates of those burned at the stake, dead or alive, during the 300 years of the Spanish Inquisition range from 30,000 to 50,000. For details, see Llorente, *Historia Critica de la Inquisicion de Espana*, 1980; Thomson and 'Ata'ur-Rahim, *The Presence of Islam in Andalus*, 2023.

their inability to lead people who were more educated and advanced than themselves (especially in fields like governance and leadership), they began appointing many of their Muslim subjects as ministers and governors. Over time, many Mongols embraced Islam.[35] A significant number of them even took it upon themselves to spread Islam among the Mongols, Tartars,[23] and in territories extending to India and China.[36]

These [frequent and sustained] incursions by the Europeans and the Mongols took a heavy toll on the Muslims, both materially and culturally. The material loss included Andalusia, with all its riches and glories, while the cultural damage lay in the tragic destruction of Muslim scientific knowledge and achievements.[37] These losses were the result of relentless attacks by unbelievers and other barbaric groups. It was undoubtedly a time of widespread ignorance and confusion. Wars followed one another, and the world became a place of defilement and bloodshed.[38]

During these turbulent times, [many of] the scholars were killed, schools were destroyed, and countless books were burned. People began to live and fight by the sword, leaving the sciences and creativity behind. States lost their metropolises, and cities were abandoned. Most places were left empty and in ruins. The remaining Muslim territories fragmented into small states and dynasties, each governed by rulers and princes who often fought one another, shedding the blood of their fellow brothers [in faith].[39] Observing this dire situation, many believed that Islam was on the verge of disappearing. Yet truth always triumphs; it is like the Sun—sometimes obscured by clouds but never ceasing to exist, ultimately revealing itself. Those who challenged the Muslims were [eventually] challenged themselves. Although the Muslims lost western territories such as Andalusia and Sicily, they

---

[23] They are a Turkic-speaking people living mainly in present-day Russia and other Post-Soviet territories.

gained manifold more in India, China, the Pacific islands, the lands of the Africans, and those of the Slavic people, extending their reach to the Crimean Peninsula. The Seljuk rulers, for instance, originating from the lands of the Turks, liberated much of the territory once held by the Romans.[40]

The Coming of the Ottomans
At this critical juncture, Muslims were in desperate need of strong leadership to protect them from the encroachments of [external] enemies and to safeguard them from internal turmoil. This need was fulfilled with the rise of the Ottomans. The people of this new state were distinguished for their courage and religious devotion; they upheld justice and objectivity and refrained from the crimes and needless bloodshed that characterized many other ruling powers of the time.

The Ottomans endured the fatigue of war and the hardships of long journeys solely for the sake of spreading Islam, protecting Muslims, and glorifying the word of God. Their intentions were pure, and their actions were driven by a single purpose: to seek the pleasure of God by benefitting the Muslim community. For this, they were aided by God. He [the Almighty] prepared them for any struggle [they encountered]. They conquered Byzantium (all the lands of Anatolia), and in a short span of time, they crossed seas to enter European territories. They took over regions such as Rumelia and soon after defeated and claimed the lands of the Bulgarians, Serbs, and Albanians. They also conquered Greece and liberated the ancient and majestic city of Istanbul, making it the capital of their sultanate.[41]

With these successes came new opportunities and challenges for the Muslims. Many of the old kingdoms near the Ottomans had fractured into small, defenseless states, but these states were still capable of inciting riots and conflict in the region. At this point, the Ottomans recognized the need to reassess and reconsider their situation [and long-term interests] across

Europe and Asia. Temporarily halting their expansion campaigns, they turned inward to unite and consolidate their power in the Muslim world. They eventually took control of Sham and Iraq. It was then that Sultan Selim journeyed to Egypt and received the trust (*amanah*) of the caliphate from the caliph himself, who, by that time, held the title of caliph in name only.[24]

The Unity of the Caliphate with the Sultanate

Through these means, the caliphate and the sultanate merged under the authority of the one most worthy of them, Sultan Selim. This period marked the beginning of a new chapter for Muslims. This era of governance brought renewed hopes and boundless possibilities for the Muslim community, reminiscent of what they had experienced during the caliphate of Umar bin al-Khattab, as well as under the Umayyads and the Abbasids. The hearts of Muslims rejoiced, and prosperity returned after a time of despair.[25]

During this time, the Ottomans turned their focus toward Europe. They conquered the lands of Hungary, Transylvania, Bessarabia, and other inhabited regions in that area.[26] Shortly thereafter, the principalities of Crimea, Kabjik, and Tatarstan also came under the patronage of the Ottoman state.[27]

---

[24] Sultan Selim took the title from Al-Mutawakkil III in 1517 when he defeated the Mamluk Sultanate. See Inalcik, *The Ottoman Empire*, 2001. See also *Appendix B* at the end of this book.

[25] Here, the author alludes to the Qur'anic reminder to believers: "After every difficulty comes ease" (94:5).

[26] Transylvania is a historical region located in modern-day Romania, and Bessarabia is a historical region that today primarily corresponds to the Republic of Moldova and parts of southwestern Ukraine.

[27] In the historical context of Ottoman expansion, Kabjik likely refers to Kipchak (Qipchaq), a historical region associated with the Kipchak Steppe. This area was inhabited by Turkic Kipchak tribes and later became part of the Golden Horde and the Crimean Khanate, which eventually fell under Ottoman suzerainty.

When Admiral Hayruddin, nicknamed Barbaros,[28] took charge of the Ottoman navy, he brought most of the Berber territories under Ottoman rule, including Berka,[29] and Tarablus (Western Tripoli in Libya),[30] Tunisia, and Algeria. This solidified the creation of a formidable Ottoman naval fleet. Their ground forces were equally strong.

All these achievements occurred during the reign of Sultan Suleiman the Magnificent, the son of Sultan Selim. At this time, the Ottoman state reached its zenith [in influence and glory]. All the European states feared the power and might of the Ottomans.[42] In fact, no power on earth at that time could rival them. There were no equals to the Ottomans in terms of scientific advancements or civilizational achievements. The Europeans were still far from the level of civilizational progress they enjoy today.[43]

Muslim Countries Outside the Ottoman Domain

Among the Muslim countries not under the administration of the Ottoman state in Africa were regions like Morocco (including Fez and Marrakech), Sudan, Zanzibar,[44] and others.[31] In Asia, there were even more such territories, including Iran (i.e., Persia, Khorasan, and Iraq Ajami),[32] Afghanistan (i.e., Herat, Kabul, Kandahar, and Kelat), and Turan or Turkestan (i.e., Khwarazm,

---

[28] Also known as Barbarossa Hayreddin Pasha in Turkish or Khair al-Din Barbarossa (1478–1546) in English literature, he served as an admiral of the Ottoman fleet.

[29] Al-Berka, a district in Benghazi, Libya, was historically recognized for its salty marshes. Significant developments in the area began in the late 19th century under Ottoman rule.

[30] Also written as Tarabulus, it was historically known as 'Tarabulus al-Gharb,' meaning Western Tripolis.

[31] The timeframe for this passage spans the height of the Ottoman Empire, particularly from the 16th to the 18th century. During this period, the Ottomans had established significant control over large parts of the Islamic world, particularly the Middle East, North Africa, and Southeastern Europe.

[32] Iraq Ajami or Persian Iraq is a historical region of the western parts of Iran.

Transoxiana, Hata, and all the Tatar countries). Additionally, India and Sind were Muslim-majority regions that lay outside the Ottoman realm.[45] Despite efforts by rulers such as Sultan Selim Han, the Ottoman state was unable to extend its dominion into Central Asia.

As the populations and power of European nations grew, Christian states with formidable armies began to emerge across Europe.[46] It was evident that their primary objective was to seek revenge and reclaim victories against the Muslims.[33] However, their successes were limited to retaking only a portion of the lands that Christians had previously lost to Muslims. These included Hungary, Bessarabia, and Transylvania. They also gained control of Crimea and Kabjik in Europe and Algeria in Africa. Although these regions had been under the patronage of the Ottoman state, they were not directly governed by it.

Let these events serve as a lesson for those who reflect.

The Expansion of Islam on its Own

Up to this point, we have discussed the Islamic campaigns of expansion and liberation carried out by various actors (i.e., states and individuals) and their efforts to spread the faith and protect Muslim communities. We also broadly mentioned how this pure faith was disseminated across different regions through conquests. However, Islam also spreads by other means—means that historians often overlook: the spread of Islam on its own, without conquests, swords, or soldiers.[34]

---

[33] I.e. take previously Christian-held territory conquered by the Muslims.

[34] Unlike many scholars who discuss the expansion of Islam without fully acknowledging all its methods, Sami openly recognizes the various ways the religion spread after the time of Prophet Muhammad, including through conquest. For details on the battles of the Prophet, see Hayward, *The Warrior Prophet*, 2023.

Today, we see that many Africans beyond the equatorial meridian, a majority of Pacific Islanders,[35] and numerous Chinese and Greeks[36] have embraced Islam.[37] History clearly shows that these distant lands were never invaded by Muslims. It is evident that their people accepted Islam independently, inspired by the Almighty God and influenced by the example of [Muslim] travelers and merchants.[47]

The spread of Islam through conquests ended during the rule of Sultan Suleiman the Magnificent. However, its propagation by other means (i.e., on its own) continues today more actively than ever. This is undeniable proof that the true protector of Islam is God alone and then His Messenger (peace be upon him). God ensures that His way [Islam] spreads among His servants at all times [regardless of circumstances], primarily through invitation and teaching (i.e., dialogue), which is the most effective approach. Therefore, those who wish to engage in a noble struggle (i.e., *jihad*) should take on the challenge of journeying to distant lands (i.e., to share and teach the message of Islam). In this type of struggle, there are also fighters and martyrs, just as in battlefield combat (for the greater good of humanity). For those who travel to remote and unfamiliar places face immense difficulties in spreading Islam. Such a person is also considered a warrior, and if he dies or is killed [while propagating his faith], he attains the status of a martyr. In either case, he achieves felicity in both this world and the next, receiving his reward from God.

Efforts like these have been ongoing for a very long time, and perhaps they are occurring more frequently now than ever before. This is evidenced by the fact that this beautiful faith continues to spread and grow daily, even reaching remote areas in Asia and

---

[35] Islam has been in some parts of Oceania since the 17th century.
[36] Here the author refers to the regions previously controlled by the Chinese, Greeks, and others.
[37] This was also the case with Indonesia and Malaysia.

THE EXPANSION OF ISLAM

Africa. There are instances in which entire communities accept Islam in a single day.[38]

Today, there may even be Muslim-populated areas unknown to us.[39] European explorers, for example, have ventured into relatively uncharted regions, such as parts of southern Africa, China, and the Pacific Islands, expecting to find idolaters or heathens, only to discover that the inhabitants were Muslim.

It is likely that the global Muslim population is far higher than what geographers and historians project. This is because Islam grows rapidly without force or fighting. Many people go to bed as non-believers and wake up as Muslims.[40] Wherever the light of Islam shines, disbelief (*kufr*) fades away. This light achieves its transformation gently, much like snow melting under the warmth of the spring sun. With this [new beginning], roses of knowledge, kindness, and justice bloom. Cities become adorned, and people are enriched and beautified by the perfect human example embodied in Islam—one of the outcomes of this faith.[41]

Before Islam, many of these people were cruel and devoid of human values. Some even consumed human flesh, lived like cattle, attacked strangers and travelers, engaged in prostitution, and denigrated their women and daughters. They refused to work for their sustenance, instead resorting to deception and robbery. They lived in a state of utter impurity, despised by anyone who came across them.[48]

---

[38] This observation can likewise be seen in our times. As a case in point, according to Mohamed and Sciupac, in the U.S. alone in recent years, "the number of American Muslims has been growing steadily, by around 100,000 annually." See Pew Research Center, 2018.
[39] This certainly might have been the case during the time of the author.
[40] This literally means that some people are non-Muslim one day and accept Islam the next.
[41] This is derived from the hadith, "Islam came to perfect or refine human character," as recorded in *Musnad Ahmad*.

After accepting Islam, however, these same people underwent a profound transformation. Their mindset changed completely. Today, they live civilized lives, adorned with values of kindness and education. They are honest and generous, taking care of strangers and voyagers, and honoring guests (*musafirs*). They earn their livelihood through hard work, doing good, and avoiding evil. They live in harmony, educate themselves, and are creative and productive. They actively work to eradicate societal impurities, becoming pure and transparent. Whoever meets them now admires their way of life.[49]

If one had seen these people before Islam, it would be inconceivable to believe they were the same individuals. They once resembled brutes but are now an honored people. By God, this transformation is nothing short of one of the great miracles of Islam.

The Greatness of Islam

My intention here is not to boast or exaggerate in describing the greatness of our faith, but the facts themselves are truly remarkable. Even unbelieving European travelers who visited some of the most remote places [in the Muslim world] have acknowledged these realities. Here, I present a testimony from one such English traveler who said:

Verily, Islam is the religion which cleanses the earth from idols and idolatry. It forbids the sacrifice of people and the eating of their flesh. It guarantees the rights of women and limits polygamy to lawful and reasonable bounds. It strengthens family ties; the enslaved person becomes a family member of their former owner and is granted many opportunities [to gain their freedom]. Islam purifies morality through its strong foundation, such as obligatory prayers, charity, honoring the guest, and safeguarding the traveler. It sows justice, equality, and sincerity in the hearts of people. It teaches rulers that, like those they govern, they also have duties and responsibilities to fulfill. It builds societies on sound foundations, deters tyrants with the fear of God, and consoles the afflicted and the poor with mercy, promises of His reward, and felicity in the Hereafter. These acts of kindness are but some of the many blessings Islam conveys when it takes over uncivilized people.[42]

Other objective European writers have also attested to these truths during their travels. One such example is a treatise written by a British friar, sent to Africa by a London-based organization established to propagate Christianity. After spending about twenty years in the cities of the Maghreb, striving to spread Christianity among African people, he concluded that the people of these lands were unlikely to accept Christianity. Even those who converted, whether by force or voluntarily, represented a

---

[42] No cited source is found to know which document the author is referring to. However, whoever its author is, this particular paragraph highlighting Islam's ethical and societal contributions reflects the observations of several non-Muslim scholars and travelers from the 19th and early 20th centuries. Many of these figures, while coming from diverse backgrounds, acknowledged Islam's transformative impact on societies, emphasizing its moral clarity, justice, and communal values. Edward William Lane, in his *Manners and Customs of the Modern Egyptians* (1836), admired how Islamic practices like prayer and charity strengthened morality and family ties. Similarly, Thomas Arnold, in *The Preaching of Islam* (1896), praised Islam's role in eradicating idolatry and human sacrifice while uplifting women and enslaved people. Richard Francis Burton, in his accounts of the Islamic world, respected the spiritual discipline and communal cohesion fostered by the faith. While Sir William Muir and George Sale were more critical in their writings, both acknowledged the societal and legal reforms introduced by Islam. C. Snouck Hurgronje, during his time in Makkah, emphasized the practical and moral strengths of Islamic culture, while John William Draper highlighted Islam's role in eliminating barbaric pre-Islamic practices and fostering justice and knowledge. These scholars, despite varying degrees of bias, could not ignore Islam's profound ability to transform societies into moral and productive communities. Their works remain valuable testimonies to the enduring ethical and social contributions of Islam. See Daniel, *Islam and the West*, 2009.

very small fraction and often did not abandon their former pagan traditions or barbaric practices.[43] Unfortunately, many of them remained in worse conditions than before.

Islam, however, was voluntarily accepted in many of these places, transforming societies through education and moral reform at an incredible pace. In a letter, the aforementioned friar candidly explained this, urging Europeans to collaborate with Muslims in spreading Islam among uncivilized peoples if they genuinely wished to uproot paganism and barbaric practices.[44] He wrote, "Islam is the only means by which the people of distant lands and diverse cultures can be saved from polytheism, idolatry, and human sacrifice, as Christianity is ill-equipped to address such matters."[50] This well-known letter, however, fell on deaf ears, as European powers were not truly interested in civilizing these people. Their true aims were domination, exploitation, and, in some cases, eradication—similar to what occurred with native populations in the Americas[51] and continues on various Pacific islands.[52]

Despite their efforts, European colonizers, supported by heavy investments, special organizations, and even military expeditions to protect their friars, have struggled to spread Christianity. In contrast, Islam continues to flourish globally on its own, with increasing numbers daily. This is a clear sign of the mercy of my Lord; Glorified is He who said, "The truth has come, and falsehood has vanished" (Qur'an, 17:81). Had efforts for the propagation of Islam matched those made for Christianity, Islam

---

[43] As a case in point, even after Sami wrote this treatise, Sharkey notes that "Church Missionary Society missionaries arrived in the northern Sudan in 1899 with the goal of converting Muslims ... they gained only one Muslim convert during sixty years of work. The missionaries nevertheless provided medical and education services in urban centers..." See Sharkey, "Christians among Muslims ..." 55, 2002.

[44] Since no source is cited, it is hard to tell which letter or friar the author is referring to. See the section's Endnotes for more on this.

would likely have become the universal religion even on distant islands of the Pacific.

Historically, efforts were made to spread Islam in Europe, such as through the Ottomans in the East and the forces of Tamerlane in the North. However, the number of Muslims in Europe remained low for some time, growing gradually through expansions and migrations. Among Europeans, Albanians and Bosnians embraced Islam in significant numbers, inspired by the example of the Ottomans. Bosnian Muslims, though few in number (about 1.5 million), are known for their patriotism.[53]

In modern times, the spread of Islam in Europe has become increasingly difficult. Europeans are now divided into two main groups: believers and non-believers. Among the believers, Christian fanatics harbor deeply rooted hatred toward Muslims. Among the non-believers, some believe in one God but reject the Hereafter and revelation, while others deny God entirely. Although they may acknowledge the greatness of Islam, they do not see the need to follow any religion. For this reason, I believe that the spread of Islam in Europe is a difficult endeavor.[45] However, many researchers agree that Islam will become the dominant faith in Asia, Africa, and Oceania, while Christianity will remain confined to Europe and the Americas.

Russian travelers have observed that within a century or two, China may become a Muslim nation. Currently home to 400 million people, China's Muslim population is growing steadily.[46] This fact deeply worries Europeans, as the Chinese

---

[45] Although this might have been the case during the time this treatise was written, today that is not the case at all. Contrary to Sami's opinion, Islam is on a sharp rise throughout Europe. According to the Pew Research Center, as of mid-2016, the Muslim population in Europe (including the 28 European Union countries, Norway, and Switzerland) was estimated at 25.8 million, constituting about 4.9% of the overall population. See Pew Research Center, 2017.

[46] As of 2023, China's population is approximately 1.425 billion. The

population far exceeds that of all European nations combined, but many Chinese lead simple lives, and their current values are not resistance-driven, or expansionist in nature. However, if they were to embrace Islam which encourages defiance against tyranny and inspires sacrifice for their cause, they would become an unstoppable force.

In India, despite British efforts to Christianize the population, their attempts have largely failed, especially with Muslims. Among polytheists, for every one who converts to Christianity, a thousand accept Islam. Although Islam is not the official religion in India, the Muslim population continues to grow rapidly, as it does in China.[54]

Know, dear reader, may God honor you, that polytheists outnumber Muslims and the People of the Book (Jews and Christians) combined. Many of them are prepared to embrace Islam, and if they do, it would be as though all of humanity has accepted the faith. The eradication of polytheism is vital to removing evils such as human sacrifice, cannibalism, widow-burning, and similar practices.[55]

When European colonizers realized their inability to convert non-believers to Christianity, they turned to genocide, eradicating native populations and replacing them with European settlers, as seen in Oceania and other regions.[56] This is a grave injustice.[57]

In contrast, Muslims have never aimed to oppress or kill polytheists unjustly. Their goal has always been the spread of Islam and the eradication of harmful traditions. As a result, many of these people respect Muslims while harboring disdain for Christians. If Muslims were to establish organized efforts to propagate their faith, akin to those of Christians, polytheism

---

Muslim population is estimated at around 17 million, constituting about 1.3 percent of the country's total population. See Frankel, *Islam in China*, 2021; Gladney, "Islam In China …," 2003.

would likely disappear from the world, and all of Asia and Africa would embrace Islam.[47]

Although Islam is spreading without significant human effort, as mentioned earlier, it remains our religious obligation to actively participate in this mission.[58] By spreading the light of Islam, we can help people escape the darkness of disbelief, ignorance, and destruction. Otherwise, these lands may soon fall prey to European colonizers, who will exploit their resources and oppress their people.

These people, though unlettered, understand the realities of their situation and are ready to accept Islam if it is presented to them. They know that becoming Muslim would protect them from destruction, as Christians cannot defeat Muslims. If we take action, success will be ours. If we falter, misfortune will follow, as the Europeans will stop at nothing to achieve their goals. The opportunity to spread Islam, as it exists today, may not remain open forever.[59]

Unity Among Muslims
It is evident that everything happens for a reason, but those who wish to achieve anything in life must actively pursue the means necessary to attain their goals. In our case, the most important aim to achieve is understanding, unity, and cooperation among Muslims. Here, we are not referring to political unity or doctrinal uniformity. Political unity is extremely difficult to achieve, while doctrinal unity seems almost impossible at this point. The unity we refer to is the unification of Muslims [for the sake of God], as prescribed by the shariah. This is a religious obligation for every

---

[47] As of recent estimates, Muslims make up 10-15 percent of Russia's population, ranging from 14 to 25 million people. Projections indicate significant growth, with Muslims expected to comprise about 30 percent of Russia's population by 2050, driven by higher birth rates and migration trends. See Al Jazeera, "Islam in Russia," 2018.

Muslim, regardless of their specific teachings or the (nation) state they belong to.[60]

Just as Christians living under Muslim rule follow their own religious leaders and authorities, Muslims living under Christian rule or under the administration of a Muslim ruler should ultimately look to the legitimate caliph for guidance. In this case, the rightful caliph is the Ottoman Sultan. All Muslim countries should strive to maintain continual and stable relationships with the Sunni Caliphate. This would represent an ideological and spiritual alliance. With such an arrangement, there would be no justification for any Muslim to cause discord or trouble, as the shariah obliges Muslims to comply with the rulings of their rightful caliph. If Muslims upheld this noble tradition, true unity among them will be achieved, inshaAllah.

Muslim Populations and their Countries

Now we will look at some of the Muslim majority nations and their countries.

- **The Arabs**

Know, may God reward you [dear reader], that some of the most prominent people in Islam are the Arabs. Among them came the Messenger of God (peace be upon him), and for this reason, they hold a special place of respect within the ummah.

The Arab population is approximately sixty million, spread throughout the Arabian Peninsula and beyond.[48] This includes the regions of Hijaz, Yemen, Hadramaut, Muscat (Oman), Najd, Bahrain, and others. Arabs also inhabit Syria (including the

---

[48] According to a 2012 UNESCO report, the present Arab world had a population of around 422 million inhabitants. See UNESCO, "World Arabic Language Day," 2012. By 2022, this population had grown to about 464.7 million, and in 2023, it reached approximately 481.7 million. See World Bank, "Arab World," 2023.

lands of Sham and Palestine), the Jazirah Region,[61] Iraq, Egypt, al-Berka, Western Tripoli, Tunisia, Algeria, Morocco (Fez and Marrakech), and the vast Sahara in the lands of the black people of Africa.

The Arabs speak one language, Arabic, which is one of the most beautiful and eloquent languages in the world. Its grammatical rules are well-defined, and the volume of literature written in Arabic is boundless.

A unique characteristic of the Arabs is that nearly everyone who interacts closely with them gradually becomes Arabized, while the reverse rarely happens. As a result, their population has grown significantly over time. For example, Assyrian Christians and others in the region have become Arabized, adopting the Arabic language and script for all aspects of life, both worldly and spiritual. This Christian presence is also evident in Arabic literature.

Interestingly, many of these Christians have made significant contributions to knowledge and the sciences, often surpassing their Muslim counterparts in these fields. This serves as a reminder that Muslims must strive with greater fortitude to excel, not just in traditional areas such as rhetoric, literature, and language, but also in emerging fields of study, to once again lead and even surpass others.[62]

- **The Turkic Peoples**

The Turkic peoples are the largest group after the Arabs, with an estimated population of around twenty-five million.[49] Their

---

[49] Note that the term 'Turk' specifically refers to 'Turkish-speaking' people, such as those in present-day Türkiye and Cyprus. In contrast, 'Turki' or 'Turkic' broadly refers to the peoples of the modern 'Turkic Republics.' Turkic peoples are an amalgamation of ethno-linguistic groups spread across Central, Eastern, Northern, and Western Asia, as well as parts of North Africa and Europe. They share related languages belonging to the Turkic language family.

territories span a vast region, from the Venetian Sea in Europe to China in Central Asia, and from the Siberian steppes to the borders of India, Iraq, and the lands of Sham.[50] They are divided into many subgroups, but they can be broadly categorized into three main groups.

Group 1: The Western Turks (Ottomans)

The Western Turks, also known as the Ottomans, inhabit the Roman regions or Rumelia in Europe[51] and Anatolia in Asia (Asia Minor).[63] They are a prominent people, and their language is renowned for its beauty and purity. The Ottoman sultans, who hold the Caliphate and are the protectors of its people—may God preserve them from all misfortune—are drawn from this admirable group. The Ottomans have long been devoted to the defense of Muslims and the exaltation of Islam worldwide.

For the past six hundred years, they have ruled nearly all the Arab lands, with the exception of three: Algeria, unjustly invaded by the French; Morocco; and the Imamate of Muscat in the Arabian Peninsula.[64]

Group 2: The Turkic People of the East

This group resides in regions such as Transoxiana, Fergana,[52] Hata,[53] and the ancient Turan.[54] These areas have historically been their homelands. While they have their own native language,

---

[50] In medieval times, and later, the area of Sham encompassed the Levant and Western Mesopotamia.
[51] Rumelia is a historical term referring to the areas of the Balkan Peninsula in southeastern Europe that were governed by the Ottomans.
[52] Today, Fergana is the administrative center of the Fergana Region in eastern Uzbekistan. While the surrounding area has been inhabited for thousands of years, the modern city of Fergana was officially established in 1876 during the Russian Empire's rule over the region.
[53] Today, Hata is in the state of Uttar Pradesh in northern India.
[54] Turan here refers to the historical regions of Central Asia.

Chagatai, the Ottoman language is also used among them.⁵⁵ Chagatai is rougher and less melodic compared to Ottoman Turkish. Although there are ancient literary and poetic works in Chagatai, the Ottoman language is more associated with modern fields of knowledge and discovery.

Group 3: The Tartars

The Tartars constitute the third group and inhabit regions around the Caspian Sea and the European parts of Russia, particularly in Kazan and the Crimean Peninsula. Their language lies between Chagatai and Ottoman Turkish in its characteristics.⁶⁵

Of all the Turkic peoples, only the Ottomans have retained their independence. The Turkic peoples of the East and the Tartars have fallen under Russian rule, while the Turkic communities of the Far East, including those in Kashgar and Hata, are now under Chinese control.⁵⁶

- **The Persians**

The Persians are another distinguished group within the Muslim world. Their native homeland encompasses present-day Iran (or Persia), parts of Iraq, Mazandaran, and Khorasan. They have also expanded to regions such as Afghanistan, Balochistan, Kabulistan, Herat, and Kelat, and as far north as Transoxiana and southward to Central India.⁵⁷

---

⁵⁵ The Chagatai language is now an extinct Turkic language. It was spoken in Central Asia until the early 20th century.

⁵⁶ Kashgar, also known as Kashi, is an oasis city in the Xinjiang Uygur Autonomous Region of China. It is near the borders of Kyrgyzstan and Tajikistan and is close to Afghanistan and Pakistan, with the Karakoram Highway linking it to Pakistan.

⁵⁷ Balochistan is a historical region located in South Asia, primarily spanning Pakistan, Iran, and Afghanistan. Kabulistan is another historical region centered around Kabul, the present-day capital of Afghanistan.

The Persian language, Farsi, is a highly esteemed language in the Islamic world, second only to Arabic. Its literary and cultural significance extends far beyond its native speakers. Many Central Asian communities adopted Persian as their literary language, even if their spoken languages differed. For example, the people of Afghanistan and Baluchistan, who have their own distinct languages, commonly use Persian for reading and writing. Similarly, many Turkic peoples in Transoxiana embraced Persian as their primary literary medium.

Until recently, Persian was also the dominant language of reading and writing among the Muslims of India. Despite its widespread influence, native Persian speakers are relatively few, with their population not exceeding twenty million.[58] Nevertheless, Persian remains a highly regarded language among Central Asian Muslims and is often considered the second most important language in the Islamic world.

- **The Muslims of India**

The fourth group consists of the Muslims of India,[59] whose population reaches approximately sixty million.[60] They are divided into various groups, reflecting the diversity of the region. Until recently, Persian was the primary language for reading and writing, while their native languages were used only for speaking.

---

[58] Today, Persian, also known as Farsi, is spoken by approximately 130 million people worldwide. This includes around 70 million native speakers and an additional 50 million who speak it as a second language.

[59] Here the author is referring to the Muslim populations of India before its partition which happened much later (1947), in which the country was divided into two states: India and Pakistan.

[60] As of 2023, India's population is estimated at approximately 1.43 billion people. The Muslim community constitutes about 14.2 percent of this total, equating to roughly 197 million individuals.

Today, however, they predominantly read and write in Urdu,[61] a language that is both clear and eloquent.

Urdu has become a significant medium for communication and literary expression in India, with many books authored in the language and numerous newspapers printed in it throughout the region.

- **The Malay People**

The fifth group among the Muslim populations is the Malay people, who inhabit the coastal regions of East India and the Pacific Islands.[62] They are found in areas such as Aceh, Sumatra, Java, Borneo, and Indochina, as well as the island of Madagascar near Africa.[63] Additionally, some Malay communities reside on islands in the Americas, as the Pacific is their broader homeland.

Among the Malays, Muslims primarily inhabit the coastal regions of East India, including Aceh and Sumatra, as well as Indian Ocean islands like Java, Borneo, and parts of Indochina. However, those on the more remote islands are often polytheists or non-believers. The Muslims in these regions have their own languages, in which a substantial number of books have also been written.[64]

---

[61] Urdu is a Hindustani language containing Persian and Arabic borrowed words, and uses a modified Perso-Arabic script. Today, it is the official state language of Pakistan.

[62] I.e. the Malay Archipelago in Southeast Asia.

[63] Indochina refers to the mainland region of Southeast Asia, historically influenced by both Indian and Chinese cultures. It includes modern-day Vietnam, Laos, and Cambodia and was formerly a French colonial territory known as French Indochina.

[64] As T. W. Arnold noted, as is the case in many other places, Islam spread in these regions, not by means of force or conquest but through Arab and Indian merchants. See Arnold, *The Preaching of Islam*, 313-363, 1913.

- **The Native Peoples of Africa**

After reviewing the five major groups of Muslims, we now turn to the black populations residing on the continent of Africa.[65] These groups are numerous, diverse, and speak a wide variety of languages. Given the brevity of this treatise, we will keep our references concise.

Firstly, it is worth noting that the populations of these nations are much larger than previously thought.[66] The regions of East and West Sudan, as well as the settlements along the Egyptian Nile and the Black Nile, encompass vast territories in central Africa and are inhabited by many Muslim nations. The same is true for the eastern shores of Africa, extending all the way to Zanzibar.

Secondly, the spread of Islam among the natives of Africa has exceeded earlier assumptions. It has now been established that many lands beyond the Equator, once largely unknown, are inhabited by Muslims. Furthermore, those who have not yet embraced Islam are doing so at an increasing rate.[67] It can be estimated that the number of black Muslims in Africa is no less than 70 to 80 million.

---

[65] The authors Mubarak and Walid, *Centering Black Narrative*, highlight that the terms "black" and "blackness" have been understood differently depending on time and geography. Their work examines how these terms were perceived by Arabs during the era of the first three generations of Muslims and how this historical context can enhance understanding of who among them might be identified as Black Muslims in contemporary Western perspectives.

[66] As of 2024, Africa's population is approximately 1.53 billion. Recent estimates indicate that Muslims constitute about 50 percent of the continent's population.

[67] The case of Kuwaiti philanthropist Abdul Rahman al-Sumait is a testimony to this. During al-Sumait's time in the 1980s as a Muslim scholar and doctor in a number of African countries, he is said to have brought seven to eleven million Africans to the fold of Islam. See Al Toaimi, "Dr. Abdul Rahman Al-Sumait..." 2013.

Although many of these groups do not write their own languages, many of their scholars are proficient in reading and writing Arabic, which plays a vital role in their intellectual and spiritual life.

• The Smaller Nations of the Muslim World

In addition to the larger Muslim populations, there are numerous smaller Muslim nations scattered around the world. These include the Kurds,[68] Afghans,[69] Circassians,[70] Albanians,[71] Bosniaks,[72] and many others not listed here. Each of these groups has its own native language, but they commonly read and write using the Arabic script and often possess knowledge of other languages such as Turkish and Persian.[73]

As for the Chinese Muslims, they read the Qur'an in Arabic but are compelled to write their native language using the less-

---

[68] The Kurds are an ethnic group in the Middle East, mostly inhabiting lands in southeastern Türkiye, northwestern Iran, northern Iraq, and northern Syria. See Bozarslan et al., editors, *The Cambridge History of the Kurds*, 2021.

[69] The Afghan people, also known as the "Pashtun," inhabit the lands south of the Hindu Kush around the Sulaiman Mountains. See Lee, *Afghanistan*, 2022.

[70] The Circassian people are a Northwest Caucasian nation native to Circassia, many of whom were displaced in the course of the Russian conquest of the Caucasus in the 19th century. See Jaimoukha, *The Circassians*, 2001.

[71] The Albanians are an ethnic group native to the Balkan Peninsula, primarily found in present-day Albania, Kosova, Macedonia, Southern Serbia, Montenegro, and other places in the region. See Vickers, *The Albanians*, 2019.

[72] Unlike the term Bosnian, Bosniak specifically refers to the Muslim populations of Bosnia, known today as Bosnia and Herzegovina. See Malcolm, *Bosnia*, 2002.

[73] Note that after the fall of the Ottoman Empire and the rise of nationalism, many of these smaller nations adopted the Latin script, as is the case of the Albanians and Bosniaks.

refined Chinese script.[74] Greater efforts and commitment are needed to promote the knowledge of Arabic and the *shariah* among these Muslim minorities. It is also essential to establish long-term relationships between these communities and the broader Muslim world to strengthen their connection and unity.[75]

Today, the Muslim population worldwide is estimated to be around 200 million, may God increase their numbers.[76]

The Languages Muslims Speak

The Arabic language is the primary and preferred language in all Muslim lands, as it is the language of the Qur'an, which is read and taught universally. Muslim scholars study and teach the knowledge of the shariah in schools and universities using this noble language. Therefore, a strong knowledge of Arabic is imperative for every Muslim scholar.

Following Arabic is the Persian language, widely spoken in Central Asia and by other peoples, including some Turks, Indians, Kurds, and others. Persian is written in Arabic script and is heavily infused with Arabic vocabulary and terminology, making it akin to a branch of Arabic. Next are the Turkic languages, also written in Arabic script and comprising several dialects.[77] Additionally, Urdu and Malay utilize Arabic script.[78] Urdu and Turkish are rich in Arabic and Persian loanwords, while Malay incorporates mostly Arabic terms.

---

[74] Islam has been practiced in Chinese society for the last 14 centuries, and today Muslims make up over 1.8 percent of China's population. See Frankel, *Islam in China*, 2021; Gladney, "Islam In China …," 2003.

[75] I.e. the Caliphate of that time.

[76] This number was the author's estimate in 1884. According to a number of sources, as of 2007, Islam is the fastest-growing religion in the world. See, for instance, FP, "The List," 2007.

[77] The Turkic language with the highest number of speakers is present-day Turkish, and it is mainly spoken in Asia Minor and the Balkans.

[78] The Malay language is now written using the Latin script, but an Arabic script is also used.

Although Arabic as a universal language for all Muslims would have certain advantages, the divine will determined otherwise. Today, Muslim nations speak diverse languages, which has its own merits. However, it would greatly benefit Muslims if, in addition to the main Islamic languages like Arabic, Persian, and Turkic, other languages such as those of the Kurds, Caucasians, and African peoples also adopted the Arabic script. This is because languages using Arabic script naturally connect to Islamic knowledge and scholarly traditions.[79] Moreover, Arabic is not easily accessible to everyone, leading to widespread ignorance about Islam's principles and teachings—a condition inconsistent with the essence of the faith.

Efforts should focus on adopting the Arabic script for all Muslim languages and writing religious texts in Arabic while producing guidance and preaching materials in native languages. This approach would greatly aid in spreading Islam's light and message. Simultaneously, special attention should be given to teaching and learning Arabic, as it serves as a unifying bond among Muslims and strengthens their understanding of Islam's principles.[66] We pray for success in this endeavor and commend those working diligently to spread Islam's knowledge and enlightenment globally.

This treatise is both a gift and a token of acknowledgment for their efforts; may God assist and preserve them.

---

[79] While this may not be the case today, the editors of Muslim Heritage note that "at the height of the Golden Age of Muslim Civilisation, the Arabic language was the lingua franca, serving as the language of science, poetry, literature, governance, and art." They further add, "A major translation movement of Greek, Roman, and other ancient works of science, philosophy, and literature into Arabic propelled Arabic to the forefront of the old world." See, Muslim Heritage, "When the World Spoke Arabic," 2018; Barrett et al., "When the World Spoke Arabic," 2004.

All thanks and gratitude are due to God for granting me the ability to begin and complete this treatise. It was finalized in the Abode of the Caliphate, Istanbul; may God protect it and its rightful ruler from harm and hardship.

[This treatise was] written in the year 1302 after the Hijrah of the Prophet ﷺ, upon whom we send the best of greetings.

THE EXPANSION OF ISLAM

Glossary

(ﷺ): the Arabic *sallAllahu alayhi wa sallam*, meaning "peace and blessings of God be upon him," and is used after the name of the Prophet Muhammad ﷺ.

(a.s.): the Arabic *alayhi salaam*, meaning "peace be upon him," and is used after the names of the prophets and the Archangel Jibril (Gabriel) a.s.

(◌): the Arabic *radiAllahu anhu*, meaning "may God be pleased with him." It is used after the names of the male Companions of the Prophet ﷺ.

(r.a.a.): the Arabic *radiAllahu anha*, meaning "may God be pleased with her." It is used after the names of the female members of the Prophet Muhammad's ﷺ family and his female Companions.

BCE: stands for Before the Common Era and has been used in place of BC to denote a Gregorian year.

CE: stands for Common Era and has been used in place of AD to denote a Gregorian year.

THE EXPANSION OF ISLAM

AH: stands for *Anno Hegirae* and is used to denote the Islamic calendar that starts from the *hijrah* in 623 CE.

abd: meaning 'servant/slave of' and used in (masculine) Arabic names, usually before one of the names of God, like Abdullah or Abdul-Aziz.

Allah: the Arabic word for God used by Muslim and non-Muslim Arabic speakers alike.

Ansar: lit. the helpers; the people of Madinah who supported the Prophet Muhammad ﷺ and the *Muhajirun* (Emigrants) when they migrated from Makkah to Madinah.

Caliph: a successor to the Prophet Muhammad ﷺ; leader of the Muslim community.

Caliphate: Islamic government headed by a caliph.

fitrah: the pure and original human nature as created by God and with which every human being is born.

hadith: written narrative reports of Prophet Muhammad's ﷺ sayings, actions and approvals.

Hajj: the pilgrimage to Makkah in the month of *Dhul-Hijjah*. It is one of the five pillars of Islam.

hijrah: meaning emigration; it refers to the journey of the Prophet ﷺ and his Companions from Makkah to Madinah. It also marks the beginning of the Islamic calendar.

***Hudaybiyyah*:** a place where a peace treaty was signed between the Prophet ﷺ and the Quraysh tribe.

***Ihsan*:** according to hadith, it is "to worship God as if you see Him for if you do not see Him, He sees you."[67] To do a worthy act excellently.

***imam*:** 'leader,' prayer leader and religious officiant.

***Iman*:** the concept of faith consisting of belief in God, the angels, the books of God, the prophets, predestination and the Day of Judgment.

***insaan*:** the Qur'anic Arabic term for human beings.

***iqra*:** the first revealed word of the Qur'an meaning to 'read' or 'recite.'

***islah*:** the Qur'anic Arabic term to denote mediation or helping people to reconcile, repair relationships.

***Islam*:** submission to the will of God alone.

***jihad*:** exertion or struggle in the path of God for the greater good.

***jizyah*:** head tax paid by non-Muslims for living under the protection of the Islamic state. Payment of this tax exempts non-Muslims from military service and other taxes payable by the Muslims.

***Ka'bah*:** the Sacred House of God in Makkah.

***khalifa*:** the Qur'anic Arabic term for caretaker, vicegerent or representative of the authority of God on earth.

Madinah: the shortened form of *Madinah-tun Nabi*, the City of the Prophet Muhammad ﷺ, formerly known as Yathrib.

Makkah: the city of birth of the Prophet Muhammad ﷺ, the location of the Kabah and Islam's holiest city.

Masjid al-Haram: the mosque that houses the Kabah in Makkah.

muhajirun: lit. emigrants. Those Companions of the Prophet ﷺ who accepted Islam in Makkah and emigrated to Madinah with the Prophet ﷺ to join the *Ansar*.

munkar: the Qur'anic Arabic term for evil and injustice. Muslims are commanded to forbid *munkar*.

nafs: the Qur'anic Arabic term for the self.

qalb: the Qur'anic Arabic term for the heart.

Quraysh: the tribe of the Prophet Muhammad ﷺ.

Qur'an: 'recitation,' the Word of God revealed to the Prophet Muhammad ﷺ through the Archangel Gabriel a.s.

ruh: the soul, spirit that God blew into Adam a.s., the first human created out of clay, and which is present in all human beings.

Sahabah: Companions of Prophet Muhammad ﷺ, those who met him and accepted his message.

salaam: the Arabic word for 'peace.'

***salah*:** ritual prayer (one of the five pillars of Islam).

sawm: fasting (especially during the month of Ramadan; one of the five pillars of Islam).

shahadah: profession of faith: "There is no god but Allah and Muhammad ﷺ is His final messenger" (the first pillar of Islam).

shariah: legal tradition, Islamic law or 'path'; rules and regulations that govern the day-to-day life of Muslims.

Shiite/Shia: meaning 'party,' one who believes that the authority of Prophet Muhammad ﷺ is to pass to his descendants.

***shirk*:** associating others with God, the only unforgivable sin in Islam if the person dies in such a state.

***Sunnah*:** traditions (sayings, actions and approvals) of Prophet Muhammad ﷺ.

***Sunni*:** one who follows the ways and customs of Prophet Muhammad ﷺ, and believes that the succession of Prophet Muhammad ﷺ is to pass down to any qualified Muslim through the consensus of the Muslim community.

***taqwa*:** God-consciousness, God-wariness, Mindfulness of God.

tawhid: the Oneness of God, that He is Unique and He alone is to be worshiped, and that He has or needs no partners (also transliterated as *tawheed*).

ummah: community of the faithful; the worldwide Muslim community.

Umrah: the lesser pilgrimage to the Kabah that can be performed at any time of the year.

zakat: poor-due, an 'alms tax,' obligatory for Muslims (one of the five pillars of Islam). This is a compulsory payment and is neither charity nor an official tax.

Appendices

Appendix A: *Brief Timeline of Islam and Muslims*[68]

570 CE The birth of Prophet Muhammad ﷺ in Makkah.

610 Prophet Muhammad ﷺ receives the first revelation of the Qur'an in the Cave of Hira.

622 Hijrah takes place—Prophet Muhammad ﷺ and his followers flee Quraysh persecutions and migrate to Madinah; the Islamic calendar begins.

624 Muslims successfully defeat the Makkans at the Battle of Badr.

625 Muslims suffer a setback by Makkans at the Battle of Uhud.

627 Muslims defeat the Makkan army at the Battle of the Trench.

628 The Treaty of Hudaybiyyah is signed by the Prophet ﷺ and peace is established in the region between Muslims and non-Muslims.

THE EXPANSION OF ISLAM

630 Makkans violate the peace treaty. In return the Prophet ﷺ goes to capture Makkah but it surrenders voluntarily, and the Makkans are forgiven.

632 Prophet Muhammad ﷺ dies; Abu Bakr as-Siddiq is elected his representative (caliph).

633-34 The Wars of Riddah take place in order to unite the tribes who seceded from the confederacy. All tribes of Arabia are united.

634 Abu Bakr dies; Umar bin al-Khattab becomes caliph.

638 Jerusalem is captured and becomes the third holiest city after Makkah and Madinah.

644 Umar is assassinated; Uthman bin Affan becomes the caliph.

656 Uthman is assassinated and many, but not all, accept Ali ibn Abi Talib as the fourth caliph; two opposing camps of Muslims are formed.

657 An effort to arbitrate between the two sides at Siffin fails and Muawiyyah I (Ali's opponent) is proclaimed as caliph in Jerusalem.

661 Ali is murdered by a Kharajite; Muawiyyah I takes complete control and founds the Umayyad dynasty, moving his capital from Madinah to Damascus.

680 Yazid I becomes the second Umayyad caliph; Husayn, the grandson of the Prophet ﷺ, is killed; divisions widen; the Shia movement rises.

687-705 Caliph Abd al-Malik restores the Umayyad dynasty.

691 The Dome of the Rock is completed in Jerusalem.

705-17 Muslims take North Africa and establish a kingdom in Spain.

749-50 The Abbasids overthrow the Umayyads; for the first time an absolute monarchy is established.

756 Spain secedes from the Abbasids, becoming a caliphate of its own.

762 Baghdad becomes the new capital of the Abbasids.

786-808 The reign of Harun al-Rashid; a great cultural renaissance occurs in the empire. Scholarship, arts and sciences are greatly encouraged and flourish.

814-15 The Shia rebel in Basrah.

833-42 The reign of Caliph al-Mutasim; his capital is moved to Samarra.

912-61 The reign of Caliph Abd al-Rahman III in the Spanish kingdom of Al-Andalus.

969-1027 Cordoba, with its many colleges and universities, is the center of learning.

969 Fatimids gain power in Egypt and attack Palestine, Syria, and Arabia; Cairo is founded.

THE EXPANSION OF ISLAM

1055 Seljuk Turks take Baghdad.

1071 Seljuk troops defeat the Byzantines at the Battle of Manzikert.

1085 Toledo falls to the Christian armies of the Reconquista.

1095 Pope Urban II launches the First Crusade.

1099 The Crusaders conquer Jerusalem.

1171-1250 The Ayyubid dynasty is founded by Salahudin Ayyubi.

1187 Salahudin's armies defeat the Crusaders at the Battle of Hattin and retake Jerusalem.

1220-1358 The Mongol threat; rule of Golden Horde Mongols and their conversion to Islam.

1250 The Mamluks overthrow the Ayyubids and establish rule in Egypt and Syria.

1258 Mongols capture Baghdad; the city is ransacked and the caliph is killed; the end of the Abbasid caliphate.

1288-1326 Reign of Osman I, the founder of the Ottoman Empire.

1389 The Ottomans take over the Balkans after their victory at the Battle of Kosova.

1453 Sultan Mehmet II the Conqueror takes Constantinople (present-day Istanbul), making it the capital of the Empire.

1492 The Muslim kingdom of Granada is captured by the monarchs of Castile and Aragon; all Muslims and Jews are sent into exile from Spain.

1501 Shah Ismail I establishes the Safavid dynasty in Persia (present-day Iran) and declares Shi'ism the official religion of the state.

1517 The Ottomans take control of Makkah and Madinah.

1520-66 Reign of Sultan Suleiman the Magnificent; the Empire reaches its apex.

1556 Akbar founds the Mughal dynasty in northern India.

1627-58 Shah Jahan rules the Mughal Empire.

1774 The Ottomans are defeated by the Russians.

1789-1807 Sultan Selim III introduces reforms to westernize the Ottoman Empire.

1798-1801 Napoleon Bonaparte occupies Egypt.

1805-48 Muhammad Ali begins a campaign of modernization in Egypt.

1808-39 Sultan Mahmud II introduces more reforms to modernize the Ottoman Empire.

THE EXPANSION OF ISLAM

1839-61 Sultan Abdulhamid introduces yet more reforms of modernization in order to halt the fall of the Ottoman Empire.

1861-76 Sultan Abdulaziz introduces further reforms for the modernization of the Ottoman Empire but in so doing, he drives the Empire to bankruptcy.

1871-79 Muslim thinkers and reformers like Al-Afghani and Muhammad Abdu call for the revitalization of Islam.

1916-21 The Arab revolt against the Ottoman Empire.

1917 The Balfour Declaration is enforced in Palestine.[80]

1919-21 The Turkish War of Independence takes place under the lead of Kamal Ataturk.

1924 The Turkish National Assembly abolishes the Caliphate.

1948 Soon after its establishment, the state of Israel initiates campaigns of ethnic cleansing against the native Palestinian communities.

1969 The OIC (Organization of Islamic Cooperation) is established.

---

[80] The Balfour Declaration was a statement issued by the British government during World War I, expressing support for the establishment of a "national home for the Jewish people" in Palestine, which at the time was an Arab-inhabited region under Ottoman rule with a minority Jewish population. The statement did not call for the establishment of a Jewish state. See Khalidi, *The Hundred Years' War on Palestine*, 2021.

Appendix B: *List of Caliphs and Sultans*[81]

Rashidun Caliphs *(632 – 661)*
Main location: Madinah (present-day Saudi Arabia)
Abu Bakr as-Siddiq (632 – 634)
Umar bin al-Khattab (634 – 644)
Uthman bin Affan (644 – 656)
Ali ibn Abi Talib (656 – 661)

Umayyad Caliphs *(661 – 750)*
Main location: Damascus (present-day Syria)
Muawiyyah I (661 – 680)
Yazid I (680 – 683)
Muawiyyah II (683 – 684)
Marwan I (684 – 685)
Abd al-Malik (685 – 705)
Al-Walid I (705 – 715)
Sulayman (715 – 717)
Umar II (717 – 720)
Yazid II (720 – 724)
Hisham (724 – 743)
Al-Walid II (743 – 744)
Yazid III (744)
Ibrahim (744)
Marwan II (744 – 750)

Abbasid Caliphs *(750 – 1258)*
Main location: Baghdad (present-day Iraq)
As-Saffah (750 – 754)

---

[81] The list is incomplete, except for the Ottoman period. Note that the terms 'caliph' and 'sultan' are often used interchangeably, although their meanings—particularly the term 'sultan'—have evolved over time.

Al-Mansur (754 – 775)
Al-Mahdi (775 – 785)
Al-Hadi (785 – 786)
Harun al-Rashid (786 – 809)
Al-Amin (809 – 813)
Al-Ma'mun (813 – 833)
Al-Mu'tasim (833 – 842)
Al-Wathiq (842 – 847)
Al-Mutawakkil (847 – 861)
Al-Muntasir (861 – 862)
Al-Musta'in (862 – 866)
Al-Mu'tazz (866 – 869)
Al-Muhtadi (869 – 870)
Al-Mu'tamid (870 – 892)
Al-Mu'tadid (892 – 902)
Al-Muktafi (902 – 908)
Al-Muqtadir (908 – 932)
Al-Qahir (932 – 934)
Ar-Radi (934 – 940)
Al-Muttaqi (940 – 944)
Al-Mustakfi (944 – 946)
Al-Muti (946 – 974)
At-Ta'i (974 – 991)
Al-Qadir (991 – 1031)
Al-Qa'im (1031 – 1075)
Al-Muqtadi (1075 – 1094)
Al-Mustazhir (1094 – 1118)
Al-Mustarshid (1118 – 1135)
Ar-Rashid (1135 – 1136)
Al-Muqtafi (1136 – 1160)
Al-Mustanjid (1160 – 1170)
Al-Mustadi (1170 – 1180)

An-Nasir (1180 – 1225)
Az-Zahir (1225 – 1226)
Al-Mustansir (1226 – 1242)
Al-Musta'sim (1242 – 1258)

Caliphs of Cordoba *(929 – 1031)*
Main location: Cordoba (present-day Spain)
Abd-ar-Rahman III (929 – 961)
Al-Hakam II (961 – 976)
Hisham II al-Hakam (976 – 1009)
Muhammad II (1009)
Sulayman ibn al-Hakam (1009 – 1010)
Hisham II al-Hakam, *restored* (1010 – 1013)
Sulayman ibn al-Hakam, *restored* (1013 – 1016)
Abd ar-Rahman IV (1021 – 1022)
Abd ar-Rahman V (1022 – 1023)
Muhammad III (1023 – 1024)
Hisham III (1027 – 1031)

Fatimid Caliphs *(910 – 1171)*
Main location: Mahdia, El-Mansuriya (present-day Tunisia)
Ubayd Allah al-Mahdi Billah (910 – 934)
Muhammad al-Qa'im Bi-Amrillah (934 – 946)
Ismail al-Mansur (946 – 953)
Al-Muizz Lideenillah (953 – 975)
Abu Mansoor Nizar al-Aziz Billah (975 – 996)
Al-Hakim bi-Amr Allah (996 – 1021)
Ali az-Zahir (1021 – 1036)
Ma'ad al-Mustansir Billah (1036 – 1094)
Al-Musta'li (1094 – 1101)
Al-Amir (1101 – 1130)
Al-Hafiz (1130 – 1149)

Al-Zafir (1149 – 1154)
Al-Faiz (1154 – 1160)
Al-Adid (1160 – 1171)

Ayyubid Sultans *(1171 – 1260)*
Main location: Cairo, Aleppo (present-day Egypt and Syria)
Salah al-Din Ayyub (1174 – 1193)
Al-Aziz Uthman (1193 – 1198)
Al-Mansur Nasir al-Din Muhammad (1198 – 1200)
Al-Adil Sayf al-Din Abu Bakr I (1200 – 1218)
Al-Kamil (1218 – 1238)
Al-Adil Sayf al-Din Abu Bakr II (1238 – 1240)
Al-Salih Ayyub (1240 – 1249)
Al-Mu'azzam Turan-Shah (1249 – 1250)
Al-Ashraf Musa (1250 – 1254)

Caliphs of Cairo *(1261 – 1517)*
Main location: Cairo (present-day Egypt)
Al-Mustansir II (1261 – 1262)
Al-Hakim I (1262 – 1302)
Al-Mustakfi I (1302 – 1340)
Al-Hakim II (1341 – 1352)
Al-Mu'tadid I (1352 – 1362)
Al-Mutawakkil I (1362 – 1383)
Al-Wathiq II (1383 – 1386)
Al-Mu'tasim (1386 – 1389)
Al-Mutawakkil I, *restored* (1389 – 1406)
Al-Musta'in (1406 – 1414)
Al-Mu'tadid II (1414 – 1441)
Al-Mustakfi II (1441 – 1451)
Al-Qa'im (1451 – 1455)
Al-Mustanjid (1455 – 1479)

Al-Mutawakkil II (1479 – 1497)
Al-Mustamsik (1497 – 1508)
Al-Mutawakkil III (1508 – 1517)

Almohad Caliphs *(1145 – 1269)*
Main location: Tinmel, Marrakesh, Cordoba, Seville (present-day Morocco and Spain)
Abd al-Mu'min (1145 – 1163)
Abu Yaqub Yusuf I (1163 – 1184)
Abu Yusuf Yaqub al-Mansur (1184 – 1199)
Muhammad an-Nasir (1199 – 1213)
Abu Ya'qub Yusuf II al-Mustansir (1213 – 1224)
Abd al-Wahid I al-Makhlu (1224)
Abdallah al-Adil (1224 – 1227)
Yahya al-Mutasim (1224 – 1229)
Idris I al-Ma'mun (1227 – 1232)
Abd al-Wahid II al Rashid (1232 – 1242)
Ali al-Said (1242 – 1248)
Umar al-Murtada (1248 – 1266)
Idris II al-Wathiq (1266 – 1269)

Ottoman Caliphs/Sultans *(1299 – 1924)*
Main location: Istanbul, Bursa, Sogut, Edirne (present-day Türkiye)
Osman I Gazi (1288 – 1326)
Orhan Gazi (1326 – 1362)
Murat I Gazi (1362 – 1389)
Bayezit I (1389 – 1402)
Interregnum (1402 – 1413)
Mehmet I (1413 – 1421)
Murat II (1421 – 1444), *abdicated*
Mehmet II (1444 – 1446)

Murad II (1446 – 1451)
Mehmet II (1451 – 1481)
Bayezid II (1481 – 1512), *deposed*
Selim I (1512 – 1520)
Suleiman the Magnificent (1520 – 1566)
Selim II (1566 – 1574)
Murat III (1574 – 1595)
Mehmet III (1595 – 1603)
Ahmed I (1603 – 1617)
Mustafa I (1617 – 1618), *deposed*
Osman II (1618 – 1622), *deposed*
Mustafa I (1622 – 1623), *deposed*
Murat IV (1623 – 1640)
Ibrahim I (1640 – 1648)
Mehmet IV (1648 – 1687), *deposed*
Suleiman II (1687 – 1691)
Ahmed II (1691 – 1695)
Mustafa II (1695 – 1703), *deposed*
Ahmed III (1703 – 1730), *deposed*
Mahmud I (1730 – 1754)
Osman III (1754 – 1757)
Mustafa III (1757 – 1774)
Abdul Hamid I (1774 – 1789)
Selim III (1789 – 1807), *deposed*
Mustafa IV (1807 – 1808), *deposed*
Mahmud II (1808 – 1839)
Abdul Mecid I (1839 – 1861)
Abdul Aziz (1861 – 1876), *deposed*
Murat V (1876), *deposed*
Abdul Hamid II (1876 – 1909), *deposed*
Mehmet V Resat (1909 – 1918)
Mehmet VI Vahiddedin (1918 – 1922), *sultanate abolished*
Abdulmecid II (1922 – 1924), *caliph only*

Appendix C: *Some of Sami Frashëri's Sayings*[69]

To bring about compassion in the world, we must confront and combat its injustices.

Deal with the deceit of deceivers justly, for goodness is the antidote to evil.

The greatest wrong in life is siding with injustice and opposing what's right.

The most minuscule lawful gain is a thousand times better than the grandest unlawful one.

Our greatest duty to humanity is the ceaseless pursuit of knowledge and sharing it with others.

The happiness of a society depends on the education of its girls.

All people share the same nature; it is their civility that sets them apart.

Reading is the finest form of entertainment; a book is the greatest of friends.

A person's true beauty resides in the words they utter.

Solitude is preferable to bad company.

It takes tremendous willpower and intellect to associate with foolish people.

Alms-giving doesn't deplete the source.

When it comes to change, time is the most capable and experienced.

Perseverance and a positive mindset can achieve the seemingly impossible.

Never ignite a fire too large to control.

We often engrave people's shortcomings on copper and their merits on ice.

A minor deed, when repeated frequently, becomes a great one.

Don't place your trust in someone who makes excessive promises.

People often chase after perfect happiness in life, yet such a quest is unattainable in this world.

Appendix D: *Sami Frashëri's Portraits*

Fig. 1. Sami Frashëri on an Albanian stamp, 1950.

Fig. 2. Stamp from North Macedonia, 2004.

Fig. 3. Sami Frashëri's portrait commonly found in Turkish and the other Middle Eastern sources, date unknown.

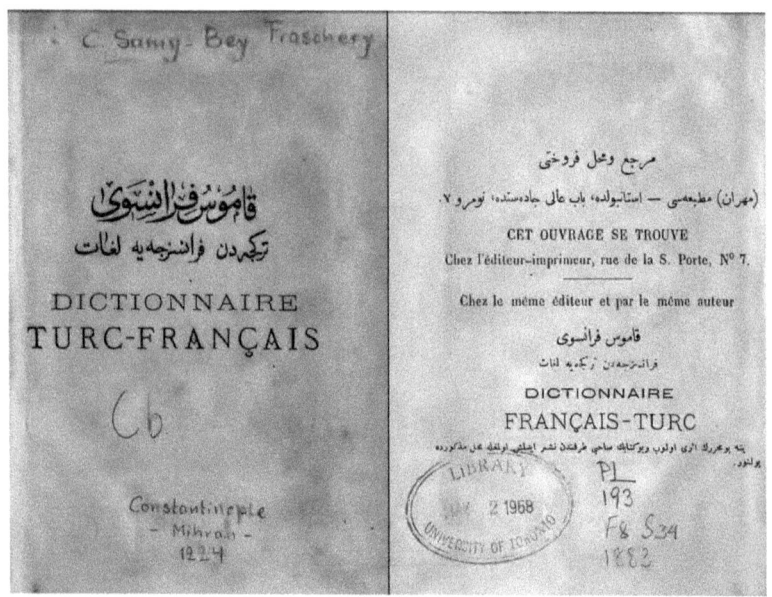

Fig. 4. Sami Frashëri's *Kamus-i Fransevi* (French-Turkish dictionary), 1883 edition.

Acknowledgments

First and foremost, I praise and thank the All-Merciful for enabling me to translate this work of Muslim history. Secondly, there are many incredible individuals I wish to thank and acknowledge for their tremendous support with this work, including my family, friends, and mentors. My deepest appreciations go to Burhan al-Din Fili, Didmar Faja, Joel Hayward, Amber Haque, Imad Bayoun, and Abdullah Alkadi for their invaluable support and friendship. Special thanks to Masud and Salma Ahmad, Maqsood and Eloisa Chaudhary, Jetmir Ahmeti, Mohammad Saeed Rahman, Kaan Katircioglu, Rania Ayoub, Imran Maqbool, Lori and David Sours, Ahmed Al-Baloushi, Mohammad Al-Rashdi, Abdullah Abu Fannas, Brian Shaheed, Stella Williams, and the following families: Offenbacher, Bresa, Yavuz, Haque, Obaidi, Mirza, Mourad, Tresemer, Jaffar, Petersen, Gashi, Govori, Carter, Peyralans, and many others. Thank you all even if I did not mention you here by name.

THE EXPANSION OF ISLAM

Notes

[1] See Frashëri, *Vepra 2*, 332-334, 1998; Frashëri, *Kamus-ul Alam*, Vol 4, 3113-3114, 1989; Elsie, *Albanian Literature*, 2005.
[2] See Levend, translator, *Sami Frashëri*, 2004; Elsie, *Albanian Literature*, 2005.
[3] Gawrych, *The Crescent and the Eagle*, 14, 2006. See also Elsie, *Albanian Literature*, 2005.
[4] Elsie, *Historical Dictionary of Albania*, 152, 2010.
[5] See also Elsie, *Albanian Literature*, 78, 2005.
[6] See Khan, *Great Muslims of the West*, 2017.
[7] This is a five-act play on the story of a man known as Seydi Yahya. See Frashëri, *Vepra*. 7 vols., 2024.
[8] See Frashëri, *Vepra*. 7 vols., 2024.
[9] See Frashëri, *Vepra*. 7 vols., 2024. See also Itzkowitz, *Ottoman Empire and Islamic Tradition*, 1980.
[10] Ibid. See also Furat and Er, editors, *Balkans and Islam*, 2012.
[11] For details, see Rahman, *A Chronology Of Islamic History*, 1-3, 1989.
[12] See *Appendix B*.
[13] See Barrett, et al., "When the World Spoke Arabic," 2004; al-Sharkawi, *History and Development of the Arabic Language*, 2016.

¹⁴ As previously mentioned, despite his Albanian background, Sami spent most of his life in the heart of the Ottoman Empire, Istanbul, where he lived and worked until his final days. See Frashëri, *Vepra*. 7 vols., 2024.
¹⁵ See Ibn Ishaq, *The Life Of Muhammad*, 2004; at-Tabari, *The History of al-Tabari*, 1989-2007.
¹⁶ For details, see Nadwi, *Islam and the World*, 2005.
¹⁷ See, for instance, Nasr, editor, *The Study Quran*, 2015.
¹⁸ See, for instance, Arnold, *The Preaching of Islam*, 1913; Kennedy, *The Great Arab Conquests*, 2008; Hodgson, *The Venture of Islam*, 3 vols., 1974.
¹⁹ See, for instance, Hodgson, *The Venture of Islam*, 3 vols., 1974.
²⁰ See, for instance, As-Suyuti, *The History of the Khalifahs*, 1995.
²¹ See Goodrich, *A Pictorial Geography Of The World*, 436, 1854.
²² Although written decades after Sami wrote the treaties at hand, T. W. Arnold provides a strikingly similar introduction to this topic in his *The Preaching of Islam*, 10-16, 1913.
²³ See Frashëri, *Vepra*. 7 vols., 2024, where Frashëri mentions the events in detail. See also Frankel, *Islam in China*, 2021; Gladney, "Islam in China ...," 2003.
²⁴ Arnold, *The Preaching of Islam*, 1913; Kennedy, *The Great Arab Conquests*, 2008; Hodgson, *The Venture of Islam*, 3 vols., 1974. See also al-Tabari, *The History of al-Tabari*, 1989-2007.
²⁵ See Masood, *Science and Islam*, 2009. See also Turner, *Science in Medieval Islam*, 1997. As a point in case, a recent article in *The Irish Independent* shows that a newly discovered ancient book proves a link between Irish doctors and Islamic civilization, adding "It revealed that Irish doctors in the 1400s were exploiting medical knowledge from [Islamic] Persia," the works of Ibn Sina

(Avicena), specifically, and others. See Reigel, "Ancient Book …" 2019.

[26] See Graham, *How Islam Created the Modern World*, 2006.

[27] See *Vepra 1*, 287- 289, 1988.

[28] See Al-Hassani, editor, *1001 Inventions*, 2012; Firas, *Lost Islamic History*, 2017. See also De Bustinza, "How Early Islamic Science Advanced Medicine," 2016.

[29] See Marozzi, *Baghdad: City of Peace, City of Blood*, 2014.

[30] See Gardner, director, "Cities of Light," 2007.

[31] See Copestake, director, "When the Moors Ruled in Europe," 2008; Thomson and 'Ata'ur-Rahim, *The Presence of Islam in Andalus*, 2023.

[32] I.e. the Crusades. See Armstrong, *Holy War*, 2001.

[33] For details, see Carr, *Blood and Faith: The Purging of Muslim Spain*, 2009; Gardner, director, "Cities of Light," 2007.

[34] See, for instance, Ansary, *Destiny Disrupted*, 2009.

[35] See, for instance, Vehapi, *Berke Khan of the Golden Horde*, 2024.

[36] As T. W. Arnold notes, Muslims were present in China from the time of the Tang dynasty, 618–907 C.E. See Arnold, *The Preaching of Islam*, 255-294, 1913; Frankel, *Islam in China*, 2021.

[37] See Firas, *Lost Islamic History*, 2017.

[38] For details, see Armstrong, *Fields of Blood*, 2014.

[39] See Nadwi, *Islam and the World*, 2005.

[40] See İnalcık, *The Ottoman Empire*, 2001.

[41] Formerly known as Constantinople. See Hughes, *Istanbul: A Tale of Three Cities*, 2017.

[42] See Reston, *Defenders of the Faith*, 2010.

[43] See Graham, *How Islam Created the Modern World*, 2006.

[44] Zanzibar is a semi-autonomous region of Tanzania. It is composed of the Zanzibar Archipelago in the Indian Ocean.

⁴⁵ See Frashëri, *Vepra 1*, 287-289, 1998.
⁴⁶ For details, see Reston, *Defenders of the Faith*, 2010.
⁴⁷ For details, see Arnold, *The Preaching of Islam*, 1913.
⁴⁸ See, for instance, the first chapter of Nadwi, *Islam and the World*, 2005.
⁴⁹ For evidence on some of these major changes, see Esposito, *Islam: The Straight Path*, 2016.
⁵⁰ I.e. uprooting polytheism. As for the letter in question, it is difficult to discern which document Sami is referring to as there could have been a number of letters with a similar message. An example in point is a letter written by Canon Isaac Taylor, an outspoken British priest; however, his letter had officially become public three years after Sami published this treatise. Though an Islamophobe himself, in 1887, Taylor had argued that Islam "is eminently adapted to be a civilizing and elevating religion for barbarous tribes [in Africa]" and that Islam had been more successful than Christianity in "civilizing" and ridding that continent of paganism, devil worship, human sacrifice, fetishism, infanticide, bad hygiene, and much else. Taylor's talk on the matter had caused an uproar in the church conference in Wolverhampton for his positive comments on Islam. Prasch, "Which God for Africa …" 51-73, 1989. See also Thomas Arnold, in *The Preaching of Islam*, who highlighted Islam's role in eradicating idolatry and human sacrifice.
⁵¹ See Ostler, *Surviving Genocide*, 2019.
⁵² For a detailed account on the history of the Pacific Islands, and European colonization, see Fischer, *A History of the Pacific Islands*, 2013.
⁵³ In our time, according to recent surveys, over 50 percent of the

Bosnian population are Muslim. See "CIA: The World FactBook," 2018.

[54] See Frankel, *Islam in China*, 2021; Gladney, "Islam In China …," 2003.

[55] For more on the *suttee* practice, see Stein, "Women to Burn: Suttee as a Normative Institution," 1978.

[56] See, among others, Ostler, *Surviving Genocide*, 2019.

[57] See, for instance, Zinn, *A People's History of the United States*, 2015.

[58] See Qur'an 3:104; 16:125; 41:33.

[59] It is difficult to discern what events the author is alluding to here.

[60] Here the author might be referring to the four schools of thought, or more broadly the Sunni and Shia divisions.

[61] Formerly known as Jazirah Canton.

[62] See Reigel, "Ancient Book …" 2019.

[63] See Finkel, *Osman's Dream*, 2007; Inalcik, *The Ottoman Empire*, 2001.

[64] See, for instance, Inalcik, *The Ottoman Empire*, 2001.

[65] See, for instance, Pereltsvaig, *Languages of the World*, 2023.

[66] On the beauty of Arabic, the language of the Qur'an, see Saeh, *The Miraculous Language of the Qur'an: Evidence of Divine Origin*, 2015.

[67] Hadith in *Sahih al-Bukhari*, book 65, hadith 299.

[68] Timeline is from Vehapi, *Peace and Conflict Resolution in Islam*, 2016, with some modifications.

[69] All quotes are from Vehapi, *The World According to Sami Frashëri*, 2024.

THE EXPANSION OF ISLAM

Bibliography and Suggested Readings

Books

Al-Hassani, Salim T. S. *1001 Inventions: The Enduring Legacy of Muslim Civilization.* National Geographic, 2012.

Alkhateeb, Firas. *Lost Islamic History: Reclaiming Muslim Civilisation from the Past.* C. Hurst & Co., 2017.

Ansary, Tamim. *Destiny Disrupted: A History of the World Through Islamic Eyes.* PublicAffairs, 2009.

Armstrong, Karen. *Fields of Blood: Religion and the History of Violence.* Knopf, 2014.

___. *Holy War: The Crusades and Their Impact on Today's World.* Anchor Books, 2001.

___. *Islam: A Short History.* Modern Library, 2000.

Arnold, T. W. *The Preaching of Islam.* Constable & Company LTD, 1913.

Barrett, Paul et al. *When the World Spoke Arabic. The Golden Age of*

Arab Civilization. Films for the Humanities & Sciences, 2004.

Bashier, Zakaria. *War and Peace in the Life of Prophet Muhammad.* The Islamic Foundation, 2016.

Bozarslan, Hamit, et al., editors. *The Cambridge History of the Kurds.* Cambridge University Press, 2021.

Carr, Matthew. *Blood and Faith: The Purging of Muslim Spain.* The New Press, 200

Dağlıoğlu, Hikmet Turhan. *Semsettin Sami Bey: hayatı ve eserleri.* Resimli Ay Matbaası, 1934.

Daniel, Norman. *Islam and the West: The Making of an Image.* Oneworld Publications, 2009.

Elsie, Robert. *Albanian Literature: A Short History.* I.B. Tauris, 2005.

___. *Historical Dictionary of Albania* (2nd Ed.). Scarecrow Press, 2010. Finkel, Caroline. *Osman's Dream.* Basic Books, 2007.

Fischer , Steven R. *A History of the Pacific Islands.* Red Globe Press, 2013.

Frashëri, Şemseddin Sami. *Himmetül-Himem fi Neshril-Islam.* Mihran Matbaası, 1884/5.

___. *Islamiyetin Yayılması İçin Yapılan Çalışmalar.* Edited by Remzi Demir, Gündoğan Yayınları, 1997.

___. *Medeniyyet-i İslamiyye,* (Cep Kütüphanesi, Aded: 1), Mihran Matbaası, 1879.

___. *Medeniyyet-i İslâmiyye*. Prepared by Remzi Demir, Osmanlı Klasikleri, Gündoğan Yayınları, 1996.

___. *Përpjekjet e Heronjëve në Përhapjen E Islamit*. Trans. I. Ahmedi. Logos-A, 2003.

___. *Qyteterimi Islam*. N. T. Logos-A, 2009.

___. *Vepra*. 7 vols., Logos-A, 2024.

Frashëri, Sami, and Zija Xholi, et al. *Vepra 1 & 2*. Shtypshkronja e Re Tiranë, 1988.

Furat, Ayse Z. & Hamit Er (Eds). *Balkans and Islam: Encounter, Transformation, Discontinuity, Continuity*. Cambridge Scholars Publishing, 2012.

Gawrych, George Walter. *The Crescent And The Eagle*. I.B. Tauris, 2006.

Goodrich, Samuel G. *A Pictorial Geography Of The World*. C.D. Strong, 1854.

Graham, Mark. *How Islam Created The Modern World*. Amana Publications, 2006.

Hayward, Joel. *The Warrior Prophet: Muhammad and War*. Claritas Books, 2023.

Hodgson, Marshall G. S. *The Venture of Islam: Conscience and History in a World Civilization*. 3 vols. University of Chicago Press, 1974.

Hughes, Bettany. *Istanbul: A Tale of Three Cities*. Da Capo Press, 2017.

Ibn Ishaq, Muhammad. *The Life Of Muhammad*. Trans. by A. Guillaume. Oxford University Press, 2004.

İnalcık, Halil. *The Ottoman Empire: 1300-1600*. Phoenix, 2001.

Itzkowitz, Norman. *Ottoman Empire and Islamic Tradition*. Phoenix Book, 1980.

Jaimoukha, Amjad. *The Circassians: A Handbook*. Routledge, 2001.

Khan, Muhammad Mojlum. *Great Muslims Of The West*. Kube Publishing Ltd, 2017.

Karabell, Zachary. *Peace Be Upon You*. Vintage Books, 2017.

Kennedy, Hugh. *The Great Arab Conquests: How the Spread of Islam Changed the World We Live In*. Da Capo Press, 2007.

Lee, Jonathan L. *Afghanistan: A History from 1260 to the Present*. Expanded and Updated ed., Reaktion Books, 2022.

Levend, Agâh Sirri. *Türk Dilinde Gelişme ve Sadeleşme Evreleri*. Türk Tarih Kurumu, 1960.

___. *Kamus-ul Alam: Tarih Ve Cografya Lugati Ve Tabir-I Esahhiyle Kaffe-yi Esma-yi Hassa-yi Camidir*. Mihran Matbaası, 1889.

___. "Lisan ve Edebiyatımız" *Tercüman-I Hakikat ve Musavver Servet-I Fünün, Kırkambar ve Alem Matbaaları*. Mihran Matbaası, 1889.

Llorente, J. A. *Historia Critica de la Inquisicion de Espana.* Hiperión, 1980.

Lowney, Chris. *A Vanished World: Muslims, Christians, and Jews in Medieval Spain.* Oxford University Press, 2006.

Malcolm, Noel. *Agents Of Empire.* Penguin Books, 2016.

___. *Bosnia: A Short History.* Pan Macmillan, 2002.

Marozzi, Justin. *Baghdad: City of Peace, City of Blood.* Penguin Books, 2014.

Masood, Ehsan. *Science and Islam: A History.* Icon Books, 2009.

McCarthy, Justin. *Death and Exile: The Ethnic Cleansing of Ottoman Muslims, 1821-1922.* Darwin Press, 1995.

Menocal, Maria Rosa. *The Ornament of the World: How Muslims, Jews, and Christians Created a Culture of Tolerance in Medieval Spain.* Little, Brown and Company, 2002.

Mubarak, Ahmad, and Dawud Walid. *Centering Black Narrative: Black Muslim Nobles Among the Early Pious Muslims.* Itrah Press, 2017.

Nadwi, S. A. H. A. *Islam and the World.* Islamic Academy, 2005.

Nasr, Seyyed Hossein, editor. *The Study Quran: A New Translation and Commentary.* HarperOne, 2015.

Ostler, Jeffrey. *Surviving Genocide: Native Nations and the United States from the American Revolution to Bleeding Kansas.* Yale University Press, 2019.

Pereltsvaig, Asya. *Languages of the World*. Cambridge University Press, 2023.

Reston, James. *Defenders of the Faith: Christianity and Islam Battle for the Soul of Europe, 1520-1536*. Penguin Books, 2010.

Saeh, Bassam. *The Miraculous Language of the Qur'an: Evidence of Divine Origin*. International Institute of Islamic Thought, 2015.

al-Sharkawi, Muhammad. *History and Development of the Arabic Language*. Routledge, 2016.

Sicker, Martin. *The Islamic World in Ascendancy*. Praeger, 2000.

Thomson, Ahmad, and Muhammad 'Ata'ur-Rahim. *The Presence of Islam in Andalus*. Ta-Ha Publishers, 2023.

Turner, Howard R. *Science in Medieval Islam: An Illustrated Introduction*. University of Texas Press, 2003.

Vickers, Miranda. *The Albanians: A Modern History*. Reprint ed., Bloomsbury Academic, 2019.

Yarshater, Ehsan (ed.), *The History of al-Tabari*. State University of New York Press, 40 Vols., 1989 - 2007.

Zinn, Howard. *A People's History of the United States*. Harper Perennial Modern Classics, 2015.

Articles, Videos, and Online Sources

Al Toaimi, Bassama. "Dr. Abdul Rahman Al-Sumait: A Legendary Productive Muslim." *Productive Muslim*, 28 Aug. 2013, www.productivemuslim.com/dr-abdul-rahman-al-sumait-a-legendary-productive-muslim/. Accessed 8 Dec. 2024.

Bilmez, Bülent. "Shemseddin Sami Frashëri (1850–1904): Contributing to the Construction of Albanian and Turkish Identities." *We, the People*, edited by Diana Mishkova, Central European University Press, 2009.

Cities of Light: The Rise and Fall of Islamic Spain. [DVD] Directed by R. Gardner. Unity Productions Foundation (UPF), 2007.

De Bustinza, Víctor P. "How Early Islamic Science Advanced Medicine." *National Geographic History*, Nov/Dec. 2016, https://www.nationalgeographic.com/archaeology-and-history/magazine/2016/11-12/muslim-medicine-scientific-discovery-islam/.

Esposito, John L. *Islam: The Straight Path*. Oxford University Press, 2016.

Faris, Mohammed, editor. "Dr Abdul Rahman Al-Sumait: A Legendary Productive Muslim." *The Productive Muslim Company*, 28 Aug. 2013, https://productivemuslim.com/dr-abdul-rahman-al-sumait-a-legendary-productive-muslim/.

FP. "The List: The World's Fastest-Growing Religions." *Foreign Policy*, 14 May 2007, https://foreignpolicy.com/2007/05/14/the-list-the-worlds-fastest-growing-religions/.

Frashëri, Sami. *Përhapja E Islamit*. Biblioteka Historia, 1415, *www.iium.edu.*, http://www.iium.edu.my/deed/quran/albanian/perhapja-islamit.htm.

___. "Transferring the New Civilization to the Islamic Peoples." *Modernist Islam, 1840-1940: A Sourcebook*, edited by Charles Kurzman, online ed., Oxford Academic, 31 Oct. 2023, https://doi.org/10.1093/oso/9780195154672.003.0019. Accessed 27 Nov. 2024.

Frazier, Ian. "Invaders: Destroying Baghdad." *The New Yorker*, 25 Apr. 2005, https://www.newyorker.com/magazine/2005/04/25/invaders-3.

Gladney, Dru. "Islam In China: Accommodation Or Separatism?". *The China Quarterly*, vol 174, 451-467. Cambridge University Press, 2003.

Hanson, Matt. "Scribes and Bibliophiles: Müteferrika to Modernity at the Bodleian Library." *Daily Sabah*, 29 Mar. 2018, https://www.dailysabah.com/books/2018/03/30/scribes-and-bibliophiles-muteferrika-to-modernity-at-the-bodleian-library.

Hughes, Bettany, narrator. *When the Moors Ruled in Europe*. Directed by Timothy Copestake, Acorn Media, 2008, DVD.

"Islam in Russia." *Al Jazeera*, 7 Mar. 2018 https://www.aljazeera.com/indepth/features/islam-russia-180307094248743.html.

Levend, Agâh Sirri. *"Lisan ve Edebiyatımız" Tercüman-I Hakikat ve Musavver Servet-I Fünün, Kırkambar ve Alem Matbaaları*. Mihran Matbaası, 1889.

Lipka, Michael. "Europe's Muslim Population Will Continue to Grow – but How Much Depends on Migration." *Pew Research Center*, 4 Dec. 2017, https://www.pewresearch.org/short-reads/2017/12/04/europes-muslim-population-will-continue-to-grow-but-how-much-depends-on-migration/. Accessed 2025.

Misha, Piro. "Invention of a Nationalism: Myth and Amnesia." In *Albanian Identities: Myth and History*, edited by Stephanie Schwandner-Sievers and Bernd J. Fischer, Indiana University Press, 2002.

Mohamed, Basheer, and Elizabeth P. Sciupac. "The Share of Americans Who Leave Islam Is Offset by Those Who Become Muslim." *Pew Research Center*, 26 Jan. 2018, http://www.pewresearch.org/fact-tank/2018/01/26/the-share-of-americans-who-leave-islam-is-offset-by-those-who-become-muslim/.

Pew Research Center. *The Future Of The Global Muslim Population - Projections For 2010-2030*. Pew, 2011, http://www.pewresearch.org/wp-content/uploads/sites/7/2011/01/FutureGlobalMuslimPopulation-WebPDF-Feb10.pdf. Accessed 6 Feb 2019.

Prasch, Thomas. "Which God for Africa: The Islamic-Christian Missionary Debate in Late-Victorian England." *Victorian Studies*, vol. 33, no. 1, 1989, 51–73. JSTOR, www.jstor.org/stable/3827898.

Reigel, Ralph. "Ancient Book Proves Link between Medieval Irish Doctors and Islamic Culture." *Independent*, 4 Mar. 2019, *https://www.independent.ie/irish-news/ancient-book-proves-link-between-medieval -irish-doctors-and-islamic-culture-37875572.html*.

Şemseddin Sami Fraşeri. (2018). In: *Encyclopædia Britannica*. Encyclopædia Britannica, Inc., https://www.britannica.com/biography/Semseddin-Sami-Fraseri. Accessed 22 Nov. 2018.

Sharkey, Heather J. "Christians among Muslims: The Church Missionary Society in the Northern Sudan." *The Journal of African History*, vol. 43, no. 1, 2002, 51–75. JSTOR, www.jstor.org/stable/4100426.

Stein, Dorothy K. "Women to Burn: Suttee as a Normative Institution." *Signs*, vol. 4, no. 2, 1978, 253–268. *JSTOR*, www.jstor.org/stable/3173024.

"World Arabic Language Day." UNESCO. 18 December 2012. Retrieved 12 February 2014. https://en.unesco.org/node/267866

World Bank. "Arab World." *World Bank Data*, 2023, https://data.worldbank.org/country/arab-world. Accessed 2025.

"When the World Spoke Arabic." *Muslimheritage.com*, 2018, http://muslimheritage.com/article/when-world-spoke-arabic. Accessed 9 Jan 2019.

About the Translator

Flamur Vehapi is a researcher, chronologist, poet, literary translator, academic, and success coach. He received his B.S. in Counseling Psychology with a minor in History from Southern Oregon University, and his M.A. in Conflict Resolution from Portland State University. Currently, he is an Education and Leadership Ph.D. candidate at Pacific University. In 2009, Flamur received the Imagine Award for Community Peacemaking. He taught social sciences at Rogue Community College and Southern Oregon University, after which he taught at various institutions in the Middle East. He has authored eleven books and translated two of Sami Frashëri's works. He has also worked as a contributing writer for the PSU Chronicles. Flamur and his family currently live in Oregon.

About Crescent Books

Crescent Books is committed to publishing works that challenge the conventional and celebrate the diverse voices that enrich our understanding of faith, culture, and history. As a small, passionate team of book lovers, we guide authors through the publishing process with editorial freedom and genuine partnership. We serve our communities by producing books that inspire, provoke thought, and entertain, creating transformative reading experiences that connect with a broad audience and open doors to new perspectives on our ever-evolving world.

Other Titles by Crescent Books

The Book of Great Quotes by Flamur Vehapi, 2025
A Breeze from the East by Wael Almahdi, 2025
Grains of Destiny by Brandon Mayfield, 2024
When My Absence Becomes a Moon by Laureta Rexha, 2024
Berke Khan of the Golden Horde by Flamur Vehapi, 2024
The World According to Sami Frashëri by Flamur Vehapi, 2024
The Spectacular Escape by Burhan Al-Din Fili, 2023
Atheism Versus Belief by Brandon Mayfield, 2023
Kosovo: A Brief Chronology by Flamur Vehapi, 2023
Verses of the Heart by Flamur Vehapi, 2021
Ertugrul Ghazi: A Very Short Biography by Flamur Vehapi, 2021

For our titles in other languages, check out thecrescentbooks.com

www.ingramcontent.com/pod-product-compliance
Lightning Source LLC
Chambersburg PA
CBHW051658040426
42446CB00009B/1198

9781954935112